UNDERSTANDING SCIENCE & NATURE

Geography

TIME-LIFE
ALEXANDRIA, VIRGINIA

C O N T E N T S

5 Molding the Face of a Planet 84

6 Climate as a Force of Change 100

7 The Pace and Price of Progress 118

1
Mapping the Surface of the Earth

Since ancient times, humans have tried to fix their position on Earth by charting the lands, rivers, mountains, and seas that make up its surface. The very first maps served as practical guides for everyday life. As early as 1300 BC, for example, Egyptians drafted maps to reestablish property lines after those boundaries were washed away by the annual flooding of the Nile River.

Gradually, cartography—the art and science of mapmaking—expanded to reflect the new lands being discovered by explorers. By the sixth century BC, Greek and other cartographers were creating maps of the entire world—or what they thought was the entire world. As maps grew in scope and sophistication, cartography became the seed for a much larger discipline, the science of geography. The literal meaning of geography—"to describe Earth"—explains why modern geographers concern themselves with everything from climate, soil, topography, plants, animals, and natural resources to population, politics, pollution, and planning the cities of tomorrow.

Today, maps continue to be a primary tool of the geographer's craft. From televised maps of a continent's weather to pocket guides of a city's streets, maps pervade modern society. This chapter explores many different kinds of maps, with a focus on how they can help us understand the planet we inhabit.

Satellites 525 miles high captured the images that were used to assemble this mosaic of the Middle East. In the center, Egypt's Nile River fans out into a triangular delta before it meets the Mediterranean; at right, the Sinai Peninsula separates the Gulf of Suez from the smaller Gulf of 'Aqaba.

How Are Maps Made?

Mapmaking is a three-step process. In the first stage, which is called surveying, the mapmakers designate a few key sites as bench marks—points of known elevation that allow them to gauge other elevations. They also specify triangulation points, which help them establish the distance between any two other points. Aerial photography is then used to chart the area, and a field survey is conducted to identify municipal borders and placenames.

In the second stage, compiling and drafting, cartographers use computers to draw maps based on the data assembled in stage one. Finally, in stage three, the map is copied by printing or other means so that it can be distributed. This step of the process is known as reproduction.

Aerial photography is a key first step in mapmaking. The photos are taken in sequence, so that overlapping frames show the same area of the ground from different positions along the line of flight. When paired photos are examined through a stereoscope, they appear in a three-dimensional view *(right);* from this, a cartographer draws a topographic map.

The mapmaking process

Two surveyors use an electronic distance-measuring device to verify map data collected by aerial photos. The surveyor at left calls out measurements; his partner records them by hand.

Bench marks—flat metal markers embedded in stone or asphalt—are placed at surveyed points in the field. Surveyors use them to verify the accuracy of maps of the surrounding terrain.

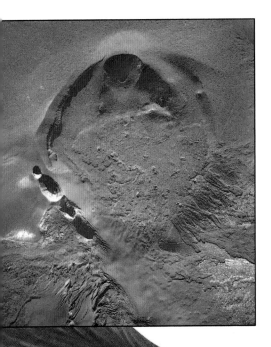

Working over a light table, a cartographer uses a knife to define the courses of rivers and their tributaries on a map being prepared for printing. Magnifying lenses attached to his glasses enable the mapmaker to see the smallest details of the work in progress.

Film plates made from the scribed sheet are passed through a printing press *(above)* to produce completed maps, such as the one at right, which shows the extent of a volcanic eruption.

What Do Surveyors Do?

Although aerial surveys are the backbone of modern maps, surveyors still need to touch ground in order to determine the location and boundaries of the area being mapped. During this field survey, as it is called, the surveyors measure distances, elevations, and directions—the three basic components of an accurate map.

The simplest way to gauge distance in the field is with a steel tape measure. But tape measurements vary depending on the weather; on sunny days, for example, temperature variations cause the tape to expand and contract, skewing the measurements. A more reliable tool is the laser telemeter illustrated below. It has the added advantage of being able to measure long distances over stretches of forbidding terrain.

Surveyors use a process known as leveling to determine the elevation, or height above sea level, of a given point. In leveling, a known vertical distance is used as the basis for calculating other elevations nearby.

Methods for measuring direction include angular observation, directional observation, and magnified angle observation.

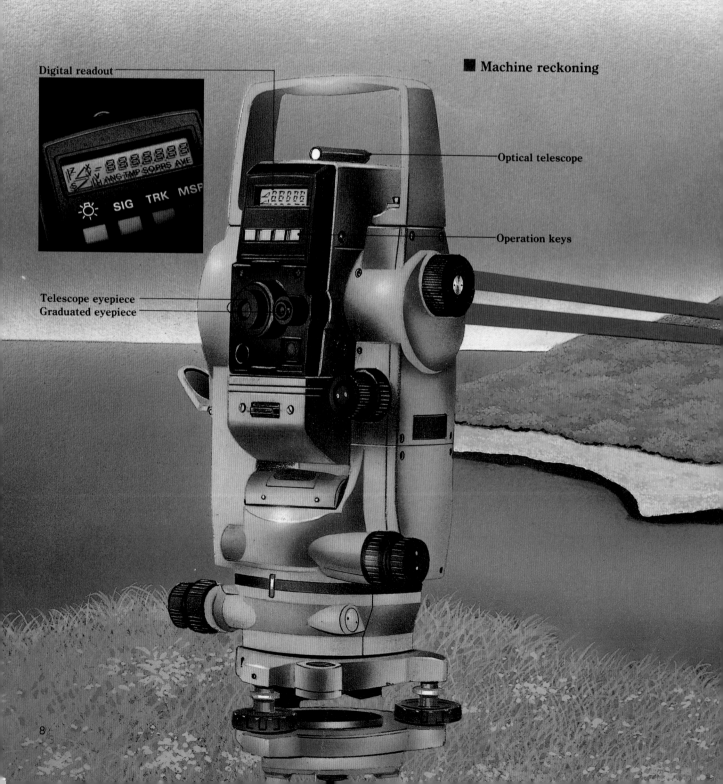

Digital readout

Telescope eyepiece
Graduated eyepiece

■ Machine reckoning

Optical telescope

Operation keys

Laser light to measure distance

One highly precise way of measuring distances is to time how long it takes a beam of transmitted light to return from a faraway reflector. In a laser-light telemeter, diagramed below, the measuring unit contains both a transmitter and a receiver. The reflector is made of several glass prisms.

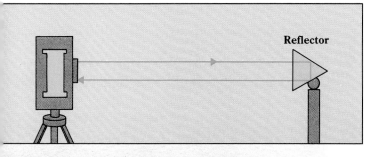

Reflector

It's all done with mirrors

To gauge distances with a laser measuring system, surveyors set up the measuring unit at a known point *(opposite)*. Next, they set up the reflector *(right)* at the point whose distance is to be determined. The transmitter then shoots a beam of visible or infrared light at the reflector, which bounces it back. By timing the beam's round trip, the measuring unit computes the distance between itself and the reflector.

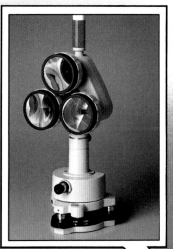

Space surveyors

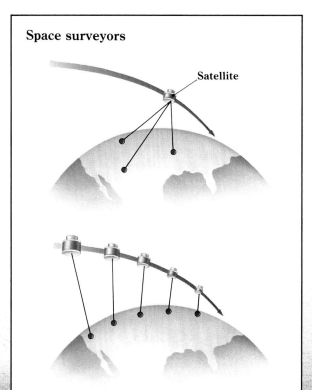

Satellite

By fixing a satellite's position, surveyors can use the craft as a reference point for measuring distances on Earth. In the technique at top, the satellite's location is determined by laser beams fired simultaneously from three known points. At bottom, single beams are bounced off the satellite from several points in turn.

How surveyors use a level

To determine the elevation of point B, the surveyor's level—a rotating telescope that can sight along a horizontal line—is placed between B and known elevation point A. Graduated staffs are held vertically at the two points, and their heights at the plane of the level are read. The difference $(a-b)$ is then added to the known elevation of A to obtain the correct elevation for B.

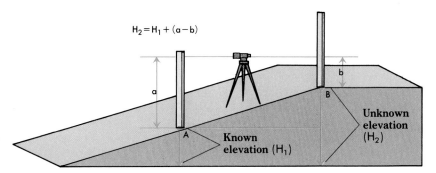

$$H_2 = H_1 + (a-b)$$

a

b

B

Unknown elevation (H_2)

A

Known elevation (H_1)

How Is Position Marked on Maps?

Most maps use a grid to show the position on Earth's surface of features such as lakes, rivers, and towns. The grid is marked with horizontal lines of latitude and vertical lines of longitude.

When a flat grid is transferred onto a globe, latitude lines appear as circles that parallel the equator. (The equator is an imaginary line drawn around Earth's surface midway between the North and South poles.) The latitude of a point is expressed as the degree of the angle formed at the center of the Earth by two lines, one drawn from the equator and the other drawn from that point. Thus any spot on the equator has a latitude of 0°, while the poles are at 90° north and south.

Longitude is indicated on the globe by meridians—equal-size circles that pass through both poles. Like latitude, longitude is expressed in degrees. The longitudinal counterpart of the equator is the prime meridian, an imaginary line running through Greenwich, England.

The celestial connection

To an observer on Earth, the sky appears to form a bowl inverted over the point where he or she stands. This imaginary shell is known as the celestial sphere. The points where the celestial sphere intersects the plane of Earth's equator form the celestial equator; the points where the sphere hits Earth's extended axis are the celestial poles. These and other celestial coordinates are used to determine position on Earth and in space.

Because the Earth spins, stars photographed by a time-lapse camera *(above)* appear to revolve around the north celestial pole. This daily rotation is known as diurnal motion.

Earth's axis

Celestial zenith

North celestial pole

Celestial sphere

Earth's equator

Celestial equator

South celestial pole

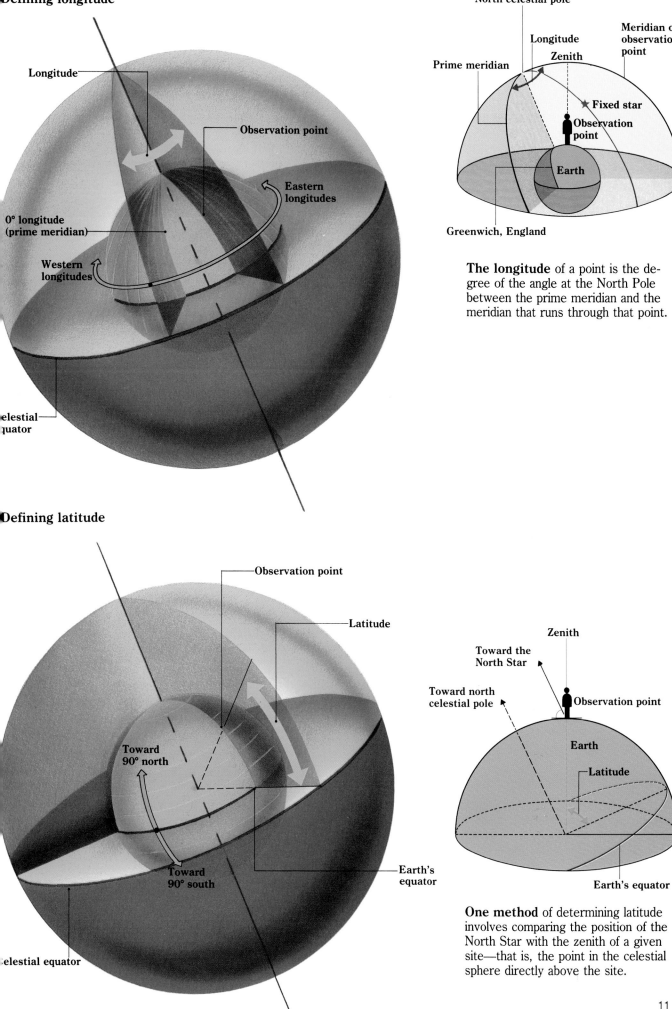

Defining longitude

Longitude

Observation point

Eastern longitudes

0° longitude (prime meridian)

Western longitudes

Celestial equator

North celestial pole

Prime meridian

Longitude

Zenith

Meridian of observation point

Fixed star

Observation point

Earth

Greenwich, England

The longitude of a point is the degree of the angle at the North Pole between the prime meridian and the meridian that runs through that point.

Defining latitude

Observation point

Latitude

Toward 90° north

Toward 90° south

Celestial equator

Earth's equator

Zenith

Toward the North Star

Toward north celestial pole

Observation point

Earth

Latitude

Earth's equator

One method of determining latitude involves comparing the position of the North Star with the zenith of a given site—that is, the point in the celestial sphere directly above the site.

What Are the Basic Types of Maps?

Base maps created from aerial and field surveys serve as starting points for many other maps. In general, these images fall into two main categories: topographic maps and thematic maps.

Topographic maps include a wealth of information about an area's topography—that is, its natural and human-made surface features. These may include everything from the elevation of mountains to the courses followed by rivers and roads to the names of lakes and towns. Political boundaries such as county and state lines are usually shown as well.

Thematic maps use a topographic image or some other base map as a foundation for presenting data that are devoted to a single theme—for example, population density, wildlife distribution, hill-slope stability, economic trends, or even local traffic patterns.

A map's level of detail depends on its scale—that is, the proportion between a distance on the map and its corresponding distance on Earth. Small-scale maps, which depict a large area of the Earth's surface, include fewer details. Large-scale maps, representing smaller parcels of land, incorporate more particulars. Scale may be expressed as a ratio. A scale of 1:63,360, for example means that 1 inch on the map represents 63,360 inches, or 1 mile, on land.

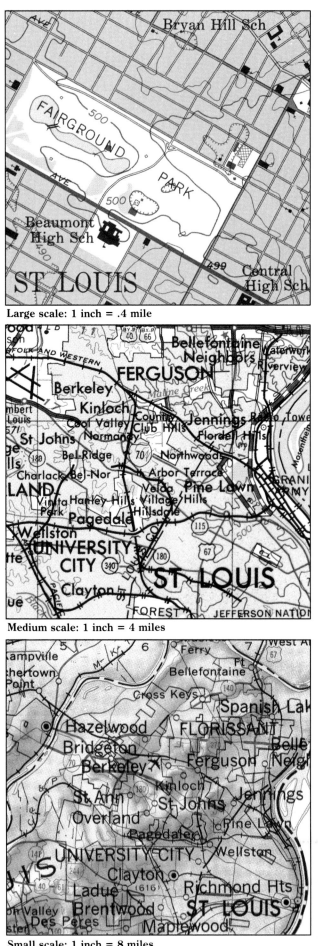

Large scale: 1 inch = .4 mile

Medium scale: 1 inch = 4 miles

Small scale: 1 inch = 8 miles

These three topographic maps show the same area of St. Louis, Missouri, in varying detail. The top map features a large scale, where 1 inch on the map equals 24,000 inches, or about 4/10 of a mile, on the ground. This allows individual features—churches, schools, even footbridges—to be displayed. The brown contour lines show changes in elevation of 10 feet. The center map features a smaller scale of 1:250,000, so 1 inch on the map equals about 4 miles on the ground. The still-smaller scale of the bottom map (1:500,000) permits cartographers to show larger expanses of terrain but comparatively few details.

Three ways to flatten Earth

The main challenge of mapping the world is that the Earth is a sphere and a map is flat. Transferring the curved surface onto a flat piece of paper—a technique known as projection—distorts the area, shape, distance, or direction of the sphere. To overcome this, cartographers use different projections to portray different parts of the world. The three main types appear on this page.

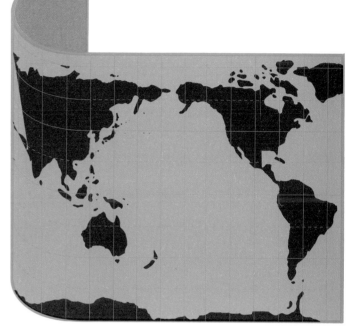

Cylindrical projection

This projection is made by wrapping a cylinder around the globe. The globe's lines are cast onto the cylinder, which is then unrolled.

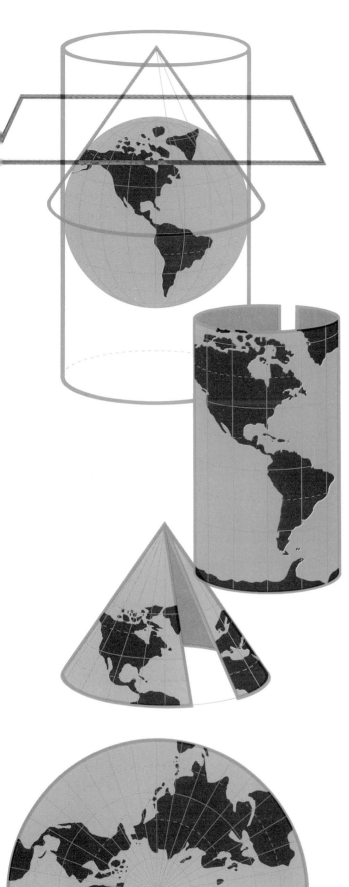

Conic projection

A conic projection can be made by perching a paper cone atop the globe like a dunce cap *(top)*. Latitude and longitude lines are then cast onto the cone's inside surface. Cut open and spread flat *(above),* the cone forms a map that is most accurate in the area where it touched the globe. Conic projection is often used to depict middle-latitude areas such as the United States.

Azimuthal projection

An azimuthal projection can be formed by laying a plane, such as a sheet of paper, against the globe so that the two objects touch at only one point. The lines of the globe are then cast onto the plane. A variety of azimuthals are created by placing the plane at different points.

Who Made the First Maps?

The oldest known map, a clay tablet made in Mesopotamia around 2500 BC, showed a settlement nestled in a mountain-fringed river valley. Its scope, like that of all early maps, was limited to people's everyday existence. But as explorers and traders ventured farther from home and returned with tales of distant places, maps began to encompass more and more lands. The oldest existing map *(right)* was made in Babylonia in about 600 BC; it locates the kingdom of Babylonia squarely at the center of the world.

Early Greek cartographers such as Hecataeus likewise placed their own country at the Earth's center. Around 250 BC, however, a Greek mathematician named Eratosthenes proposed that the Earth was a sphere; he also estimated the planet's circumference to within just 12 percent of its correct size. Ancient cartography reached its pinnacle in the second century AD, when Egyptian scholar Claudius Ptolemy wrote *Geography,* a manual on how to make maps of a spherical Earth. These and other milestones of cartography appear at right.

Babylonian world map (600 BC)

The clay tablet below is the oldest map in existence. It shows the world as a disk of land ringed by oceans. The vertical lines represent the Euphrates River.

Martin Behaim globe

Based on Ptolemaic maps, Behaim's 1492 globe *(below)* incorporated the latest geographical knowledge of his time. The American continents, discovered that year, are notably absent.

Atlas of Gerardus Mercator (1585)

Mercator's world map (1538)

Globe of Martin Behaim (1492)

Portolan charts (1300)

World map of Arab geographer Al Idrisi (1161)

Gyoki map of Japan (8th century)

Peutinger Table, a Roman route map (4th century)

World map of Ptolemy (2d century)

Globe of Crates of Mallos (150 BC)

World map of Eratosthenes (250 BC)

World map of Hecataeus (550 BC)

Babylonian world map (600 BC)

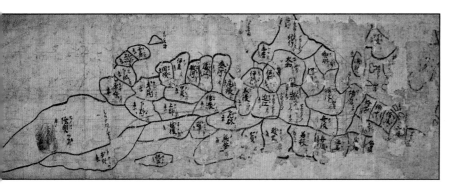

Gyoki map

The map at left—the oldest known image to depict all of Japan—is attributed to Gyoki Bosatsu, an eighth-century Buddhist priest. It shows the names and boundaries of towns and territories, as well as the roads linking them.

Ptolemy's world map

Engraved during the Renaissance, maps like the one at right were based on the second-century writings of Ptolemy. This astronomer and geographer pioneered the concepts of latitude and longitude, as well as projection.

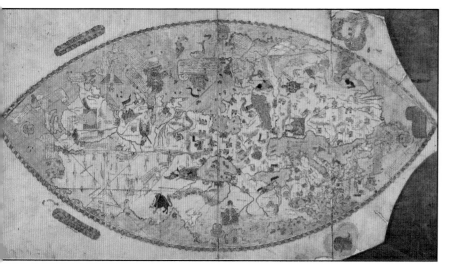

Portolan chart

The world map at left, dating from 1457, is known as a portolan chart—a sea chart that shows compass bearings. Made in Italy as early as 1300, portolans used straight lines to show the direction of various winds. The maps enabled navigators to determine the correct heading to their destination.

What Is a Mercator Projection?

Devised by Flemish cartographer Gerardus Mercator in 1569, a Mercator projection is a map that shows latitude and longitude lines so that they form squares or rectangles. The projection is well suited to nautical charts, because a straight line connecting any two points on a Mercator map makes the same angle with every meridian it intersects. This rhumb line, as it is called, gives seafarers a route that can be followed by maintaining a constant compass bearing.

But for all its value to navigators, a Mercator projection distorts the shapes and sizes of oceans and landmasses. Instead of converging at the poles, as they do on Earth's surface, the merid-

ians on a Mercator map appear as parallel vertical lines. For this reason, all east-west distances (except those at the equator) are stretched out, with the greatest expansion occurring in the highest latitudes.

Latitude lines, too, are distorted by a Mercator projection; the spacing between them increases with their distance from the equator. As a result, regions in higher latitudes look much larger than equal-size areas in lower latitudes: Greenland, for example, is less than one-twelfth the size of South America, but on a Mercator map the island balloons to an area several times bigger than the continent.

Distortion, Mercator style

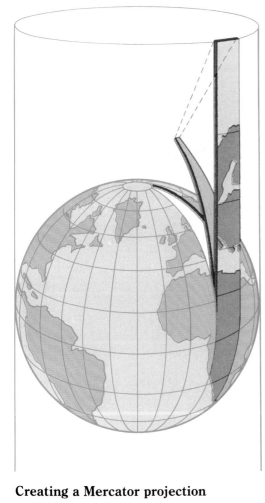

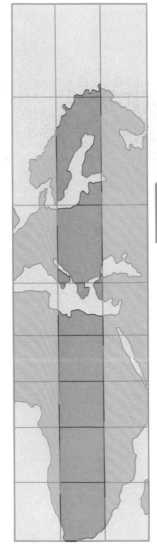

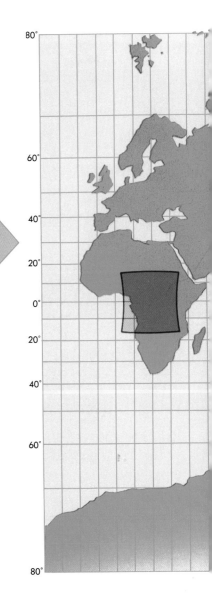

Creating a Mercator projection

A Mercator projection can be visualized by peeling from the globe a strip that lies between two meridians *(above)*. The meridians are then stretched apart at the poles, forming two parallel lines. To offset this expansion, the map's lines of latitude must be spaced farther and farther apart as their distance from the equator increases *(right)*.

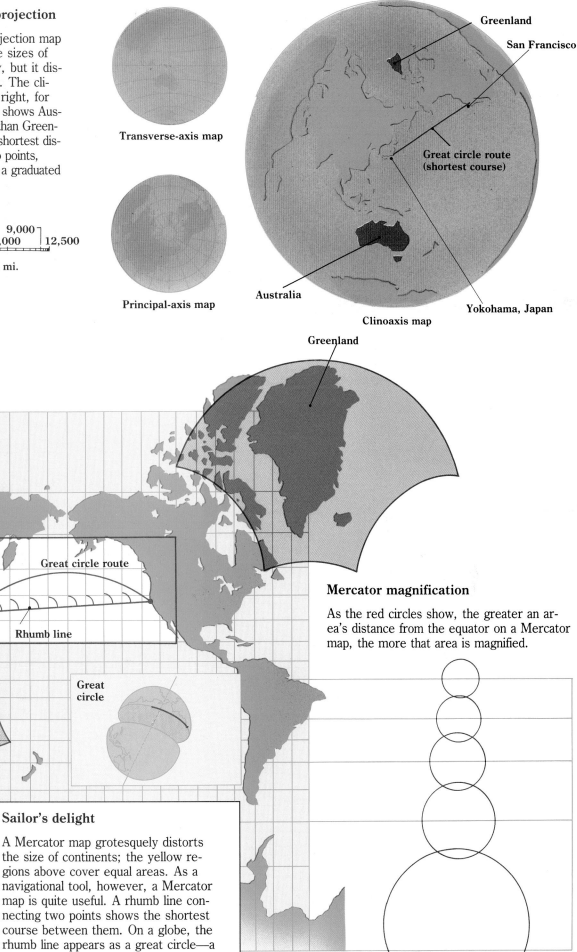

An equal-area projection

An equal-area projection map shows the relative sizes of regions accurately, but it distorts their shapes. The clinoaxis map at far right, for example, correctly shows Australia much larger than Greenland. Figuring the shortest distance between two points, however, requires a graduated scale *(below)*.

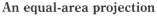

0 (km)   500   1,000   9,000   12,500

1 km = .6214 mi.

Transverse-axis map

Principal-axis map

Greenland

San Francisco

Great circle route (shortest course)

Australia

Yokohama, Japan

Clinoaxis map

Greenland

Great circle route

Rhumb line

Great circle

Australia

Mercator magnification

As the red circles show, the greater an area's distance from the equator on a Mercator map, the more that area is magnified.

Sailor's delight

A Mercator map grotesquely distorts the size of continents; the yellow regions above cover equal areas. As a navigational tool, however, a Mercator map is quite useful. A rhumb line connecting two points shows the shortest course between them. On a globe, the rhumb line appears as a great circle—a line that delineates the intersection between the Earth's surface and a plane passing through Earth's center.

How Are Nautical Charts Made?

To find their way across the sea, most sailors rely on nautical charts—maps designed especially for navigation. A baseline survey, during which surveyors establish the boundaries of the waters to be mapped, is the first step in producing a nautical chart. Next, survey ships take soundings to measure depth; the coastline is surveyed by aerial photography; and magnetic north is determined. Finally, data on tides and currents—as well as the locations of lighthouses, buoys, and any underwater obstructions—are gathered and incorporated into the chart. The chart will be periodically revised to reflect any changes in water depth or shoreline.

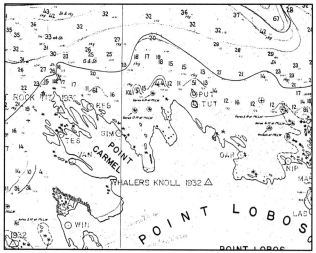

A survey ship *(below)* uses a multibeam echo sounder to make depth charts *(above)*. Depths are in fathoms.

Sounding the depths

Transmitted beam

Transmitted beam

Mapped area

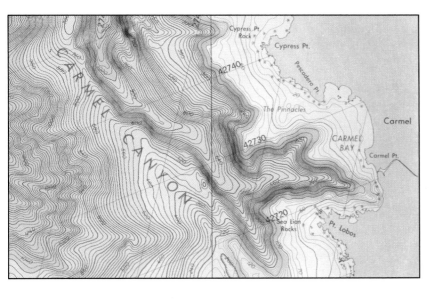

Views of the invisible

Hydrographic surveys form the basis for a bathymetric map, a topographic map of the seafloor. Similar seabed depths are connected by contour lines. Widely spaced lines indicate a gradual slope in the seabed, whereas closely spaced lines denote a steeper slope. The depth contours reveal the size, shape, and distribution of all sorts of seafloor features, from canyons to fault lines to mineral veins.

If the depth-sounding data are sufficiently detailed, they can be manipulated by computer to produce a three-dimensional view of the ocean floor *(left)*.

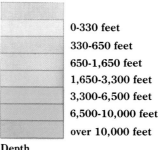

Aerial photos, such as this one of California's Carmel Bay, enable cartographers to measure the topography of a coastline. The photos also reveal the location of navigational aids and hazards, such as beacons and buried wrecks. Both types of information are crucial to a chart.

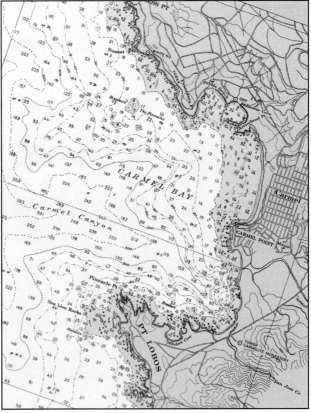

The finished nautical chart incorporates data collected by many different means, including aerial photography, depth soundings, and magnetic surveys. New chart editions of heavily trafficked areas—the coast of California or New York Harbor—are published once a year.

Why Were Time Zones Created?

Time is linked to longitude. The Earth moves through one rotation, or 360° of longitude, in 24 hours. Each hour of time is therefore equivalent to 15° of longitude, so the Earth turns 1° every four minutes.

The time at any point on Earth can be set by defining noon as the moment when the sun appears directly above the meridian at that point. This method is not used, however, because it would result in different times for all 360 meridians. Instead, the Earth has been divided into 24 time zones—corresponding to the 24 hours of the day—of 15° each. The same time is used throughout each 15° zone.

At the 1884 International Meridian Conference, 27 nations agreed to an international time-zone system. The conference established the meridian passing through Greenwich, England, as the zero point, or prime meridian, for the measurement of longitude—and thus of time. The 180th meridian, which lies halfway (and half a day) around the world from Greenwich, was designated the International Date Line. It is the place where each day begins and ends for the world.

Dawn of a new day

All days are born at midnight at the International Date Line and proceed westward. On the globe below, the new day is only four hours old. As the Earth turns, the new day will take in more of the world with every hour. Meanwhile, the old day gets smaller by the hour, then disappears at the date line.

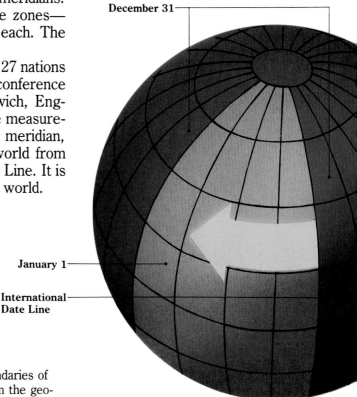

December 31

January 1

International
Date Line

The boundaries of time

To accommodate national, state, or local borders, the boundaries of the world's standard time zones *(below)* often jut away from the geographical meridians that divide Earth into 24 time zones.

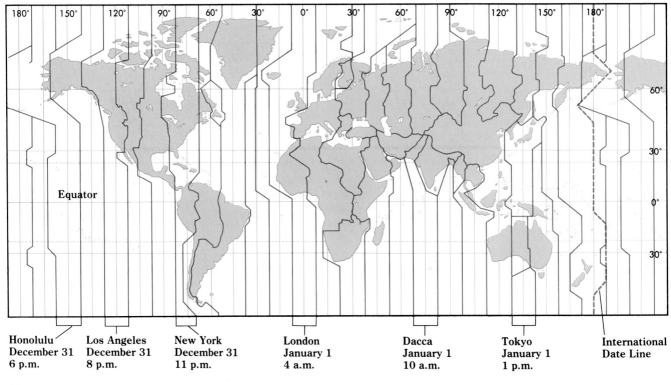

| Honolulu December 31 6 p.m. | Los Angeles December 31 8 p.m. | New York December 31 11 p.m. | London January 1 4 a.m. | Dacca January 1 10 a.m. | Tokyo January 1 1 p.m. | International Date Line |

The prime meridian—the zero point for measuring longitude—passes through the Royal Observatory at Greenwich *(left),* near London, England.

As illustrated in the diagram at right, a day is the time it takes a given meridian to make one complete revolution in relation to a coordinate on the celestial sphere.

North celestial pole

Celestial sphere

Coordinate on celestial sphere

Observation point

Date line

Celestial meridian

South celestial pole

Greenwich

180th meridian

The 180th meridian, the base for the International Date Line, runs through the sparsely populated Pacific Ocean. As shown by the transparent globe at right, the date line is part of the same great circle as the prime meridian, which passes through Greenwich.

Prime meridian

Because the 180th meridian cuts through several island groups in the Pacific, the date line zigzags *(below)* so that the day of the week is the same throughout each country.

The 180th meridian cleaves the Fiji Islands.

How Are Computer Maps Made?

Modern computer science has revolutionized the ancient art of cartography. No longer must every detail of a map be painstakingly drawn by hand. Instead, the data gathered during surveys are fed into a computer, or existing maps are optically scanned and entered into the machine. Some computers can receive digitized map images directly from satellites.

Once a cartographic database has been established, a mapmaker can manipulate the data in remarkable ways. A topographic base map, for example, may serve as the foundation for an image showing the extent of a rain forest, the areas that rise above a given elevation, or even the distribution of hummingbirds.

Cartographers also have a wide choice when it comes to displaying computerized maps, such as the views of Mount Fuji shown on these pages. Digitized map data may be rendered as drawings on a sheet of paper or as images on a piece of microfilm. Other maps—typically those depicting weather forecasts—may be projected on computer or television screens.

Where precision is king

Mount Fuji *(below),* an extinct volcano on the island of Honshu in central Japan, towers above its surrounding plain. At an elevation of 12,395 feet, Fuji is the country's highest mountain.

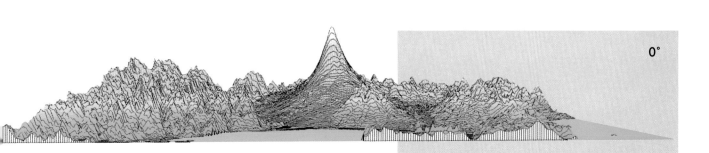

0°

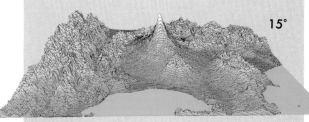

15°

Angling for a view

One of the biggest boons of computer mapping is the ability to view a landform from different angles. The series of relief maps above and at right, for example, shows Mount Fuji as it would be seen by a bird flying at angles to the ground of 0°, 15°, 30°, and 60°.

30°

60°

Computing the future

Color-coded to indicate elevation, the relief maps at right display the coast of Japan's Suruga Bay in its present configuration *(top)* and as it would look if the sea level rose 200 feet *(bottom)*. Computers have greatly simplified this and other types of topographic forecasting.

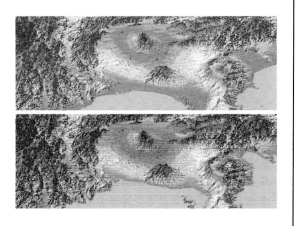

2

Earth's Colossal Stonecutters

Rivers and glaciers are mighty sculpting tools. Agents of the great cycle that shuttles water from the oceans to the air to the land and back again, they transform the earth around them, grinding mountains into valleys and paving plains to the sea.

The water that fuels their work begins as vapor drawn from oceans, rivers, soil, and plants. After gathering into clouds, the moisture precipitates in the form of rain or snow. Some of this precipitation falls on the oceans or evaporates. The rest collects on land as lakes, underground springs, or snowfields, all of which give rise to tiny channels of water, called rills, that make up a river's headwaters. Coursing downhill, the rills join to form brooks and streams; these, in turn, eventually combine to form rivers.

A flowing river grooves the terrain, creating canyons and a host of other natural wonders. The topsoil and bedrock dislodged by its scraping action are carried downstream, where they form vast plains when the river spills its banks.

In regions too cold for rivers to flow, the land is sculpted by water in the guise of glaciers. These massive slabs of ice inch downhill under their own weight, gouging out stupendous hollows that become lakes and valleys; in their wake, the glaciers leave rubble heaps that are mountains in themselves. The dynamics of river and glacier flow—and the formations that result as these powerful forces shape the land—are explored in the chapter that follows.

High in the Canadian Rockies, the red-roofed Columbia Icefield visitors' center in Jasper National Park occupies the former spillway of an alpine glacier, now retreating up the valley.

What Landforms Do Rivers Create?

A river molds many different forms in the land it crosses. Near the river's source, its racing headwaters cut deep channels in the bedrock, creating V-shaped valleys *(right)*. In the river's middle course, its slope lessens and its current slows. If the river suddenly flows onto a plain, it dumps its load of debris, forming a triangular landmass called an alluvial fan.

On more level ground, the slower-moving waters carve away the river's banks. Sweeping flood plains—built up from soil deposited during river floods—now flank the river. Over time, as the riverbed drops through erosion or ground shifts, river terraces form on these flood plains. The river, meanwhile, charts a winding course, its loops sometimes breaking free to form oxbow lakes *(below, right)*. Where the river empties into a lake or an ocean, its sediments often accumulate to form a body of land known as a delta.

V-shaped valleys —————

V-shaped Kurobe Canyon in Japan

Alluvial fan —————

Landforms sculpted by rivers

Riverbank —————

Delta ———

Japan's Ota River delta *(left)*

An oxbow is born

→ Force of water flow
→ Path of water

A river coursing through a flat plain develops snakelike curves called meanders.

Flood plain

Oxbow lake

River terraces

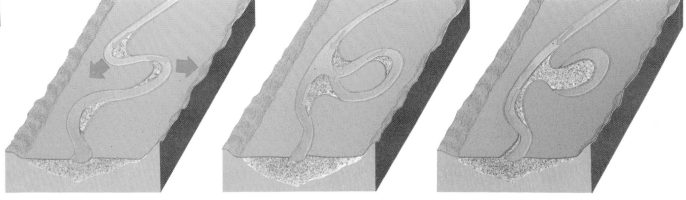

The meanders grow as water washes away land on the curves' outer edges.

Over thousands of years, a meander may curve back on itself.

Gravelly debris collects in the loop's neck, creating a separate oxbow lake.

How Do Plains Form?

Today's plains may once have been mountain ranges, valleys, or sunken seabeds. Those worn flat by weathering and river action are called erosional plains; those built up from waterborne sediments are depositional plains.

Of the two, erosional plains are far more common. Erosional plains that have been scoured from ancient rock layers are known as structural plains. Peneplains—rugged landscapes that have been reduced almost to flat plains—appear amid low-lying hills in formerly mountainous regions.

Less-common depositional plains result when a river strips away rock and then deposits the debris farther downstream. Along the river's lower course, its slow-moving waters periodically overflow its banks, creating sand bars and then flood plains. Two other varieties of depositional plains—alluvial fans and deltas—form when a river dumps erosional debris at the base of mountains or at the mouth of the river itself *(pages 30-33)*. As illustrated below, coastal plains reflect both erosion and deposition.

The seabed emerges

Crustal uplift or sea-level changes expose the seabed, which is cut by rivers.

Rivers at work

The rivers erode the surface, leaving gently sloping rock plains.

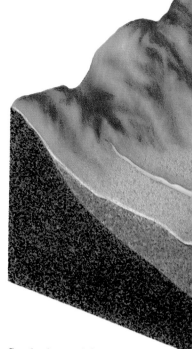

Sculpting with water

As the sea level rises, the sea migrates up river channels, forming inland harbors. The rivers, meanwhile, continue to deposit eroded land, gradually extending the plains into the sea.

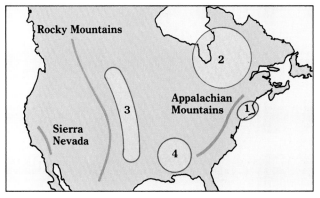

The plains of North America

Plains are common in North America. Best known are the Atlantic coastal plains (1); erosional plains such as the Laurentian Plateau (2) and the Great Plains (3); and depositional plains in the Mississippi River valley (4).

A timeworn plateau

Made of rock as old as 3.8 billion years, the Laurentian Plateau wraps around Canada's Hudson Bay. Erosion has leveled this once-mountainous region, which now averages 1,600 feet in height.

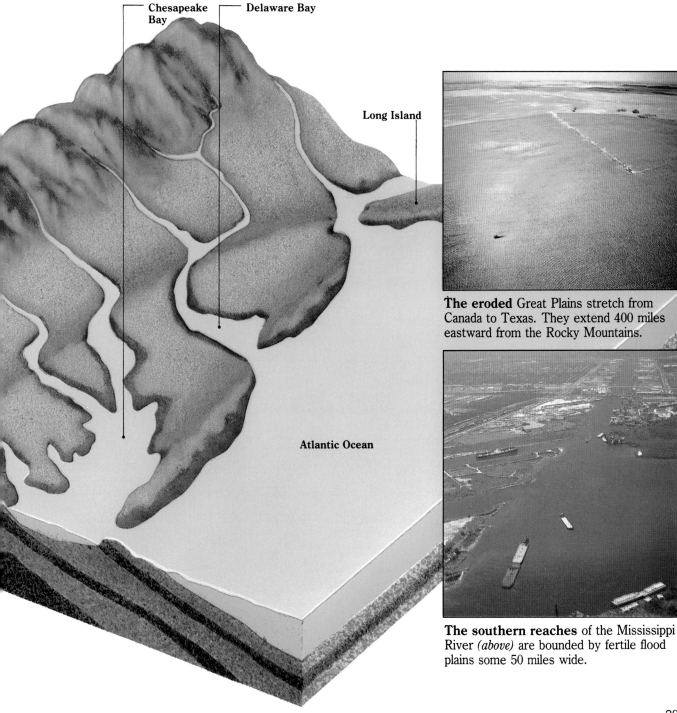

The eroded Great Plains stretch from Canada to Texas. They extend 400 miles eastward from the Rocky Mountains.

The southern reaches of the Mississippi River *(above)* are bounded by fertile flood plains some 50 miles wide.

What Is an Alluvial Fan?

The growth of an alluvial fan

Building a fanhead

Sediment *(dark green)* begins to collect where the river slows upon reaching the plain.

Downhill progress

Repeated deposits of sand and gravel (1, 2, and 3) cause a river to broaden its course. Widening tongues of new sediment (4 and 5) soon accumulate below the old deposits.

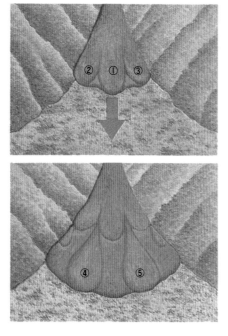

30

As a river spills from a mountain onto a plain, the speed of its current drops sharply. The slower-moving water cannot carry as much sand and gravel, so it deposits its load of sediment at the foot of the mountain. In time, this creates a fan-shaped semicircular landmass known as an alluvial fan. The top is called the fanhead; the center is the midfan; the base is the toe.

As debris builds up at the fanhead, the riverbed rises until the water tops its banks and floods out into the fan. The surging floodwaters deposit sediment past the toe, lengthening and widening the fan, and creating new channels for the river to run through. This pattern repeats itself until the collected sand and gravel actually absorb the river. Now flowing underground from the fanhead to the toe, the river becomes an influent stream. (Its dried-up surface channel is termed a wadi.) At the fan's toe, where the accumulated sediment is thinnest, the influent stream breaks aboveground as a spring. Such springs are key sources of water in mountainous desert regions, where alluvial fans have supported human settlement since prehistoric times.

Opening the fan

The buildup of sediment elevates the riverbed, sending the river over its banks. Floodwaters deposit expanding arcs of debris, and the river changes course.

Going underground

Repeated sedimentation and flooding enlarges and deepens the alluvial fan. At the fanhead, the river water often seeps down through the layered sand and gravel, forming an underground river that may then reappear as a spring at the fan's toe.

Fanhead

Midfan

Spring

Toe

An alluvial fan in Japan

What Forces Shape a Delta?

Sediment builds at the mouth

The river current splits

The growth of a delta

Much of the rock and soil that is stripped away by a river during its cross-country ramble is deposited as low plains at the river's mouth. These plains, named for the Greek capital letter delta (Δ) because they are roughly triangular in shape, owe their existence to the way river and ocean currents interact.

When a river enters a large standing body of water, its current slows dramatically, causing most of the river's sediment to settle out. Eventually, a vast pile of gravel, sand, and mud collects at the river's mouth. Blocked by this debris, the river splits into channels, each of which builds its own spit of land. In this way, a broad delta forms.

Although most deltas are layered the same way inside *(bottom, right),* their external shape varies according to the contours of the ocean floor, the amount of sediment that has been deposited, and the action of ocean waves. A bird's-foot delta occurs when a rapid river current penetrates calm waters, dumping its load of sediment as fingers of sand. Where a lazy river encounters strong ocean tides or currents, its sediments are redistributed across a broad front, creating an arc delta or a pointed delta.

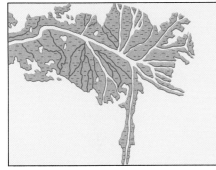

A bird's-foot delta straddles the mouth of the Mississippi River.

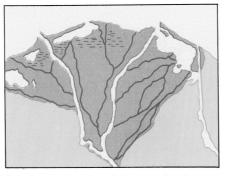

A triangular arc delta marks the Nile's entry into the Mediterranean.

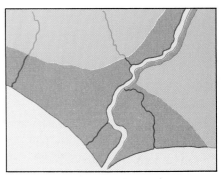

A hatchet-shaped pointed delta crowns the Tiber River in Italy.

New deposits widen the delta

The delta forms low plains

Topset beds

Foreset beds

Bottomset beds

A sedimental journey

A natural sorting process is responsible for the triple-tier makeup of most deltas. Lightweight muds drift out to sea before settling to form the lowest layer, known as bottomset beds. Sand—coarser and heavier than mud—composes the middle layer, the foreset beds. Coarser sand and gravel, which settle out first, rest like a cap over the top, forming the topset beds.

Why Does the Yellow River Shift Course?

In 1887 China's Yellow River burst through a series of dikes near Kaifeng, flooding 14,000 square miles and drowning a million people. The rampaging river then turned course and cut a new channel to the Yellow Sea, 400 miles away.

Over the last 2,500 years, the Yellow River has undergone eight or more such catastrophic course changes. On its way south from Baotou, the 3,000-mile-long river flows through the Loess Plateau, a plain made up of loess—yellowish silt mixed with clay. For centuries, tor-rential rains have triggered floods on this plain, washing the loess into the river (hence its name) and raising the level of the riverbed. Containment walls were built to keep the rising river from cresting its banks, but these only increased the rate at which the clay-rich soil settled to the bottom. When the walls inevitably gave way, devastating floods ensued, leaving the river free to cut a new course through the countryside. Today, the Yellow River follows a man-made channel that prevents such cataclysms.

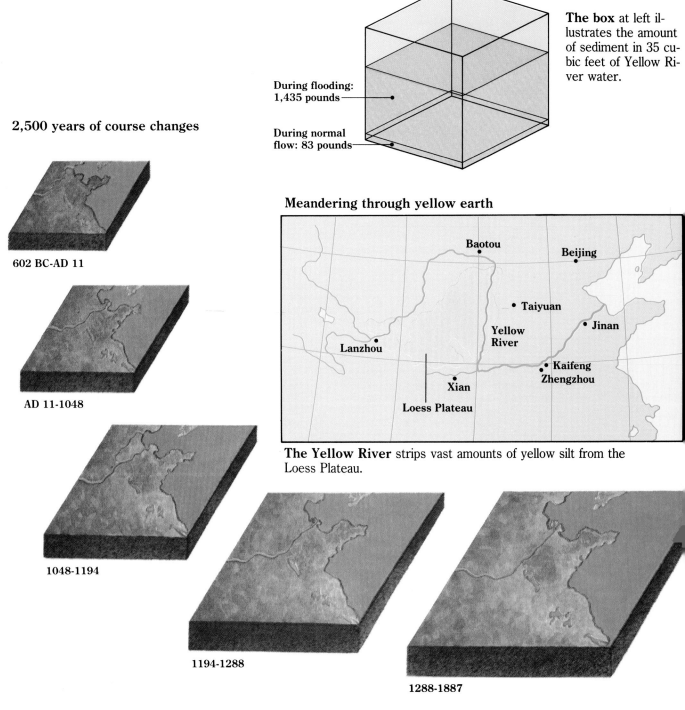

The box at left illustrates the amount of sediment in 35 cubic feet of Yellow River water.

During flooding: 1,435 pounds

During normal flow: 83 pounds

2,500 years of course changes

602 BC-AD 11

AD 11-1048

1048-1194

1194-1288

1288-1887

Meandering through yellow earth

Baotou

Beijing

Taiyuan

Jinan

Yellow River

Lanzhou

Kaifeng
Zhengzhou

Xian

Loess Plateau

The Yellow River strips vast amounts of yellow silt from the Loess Plateau.

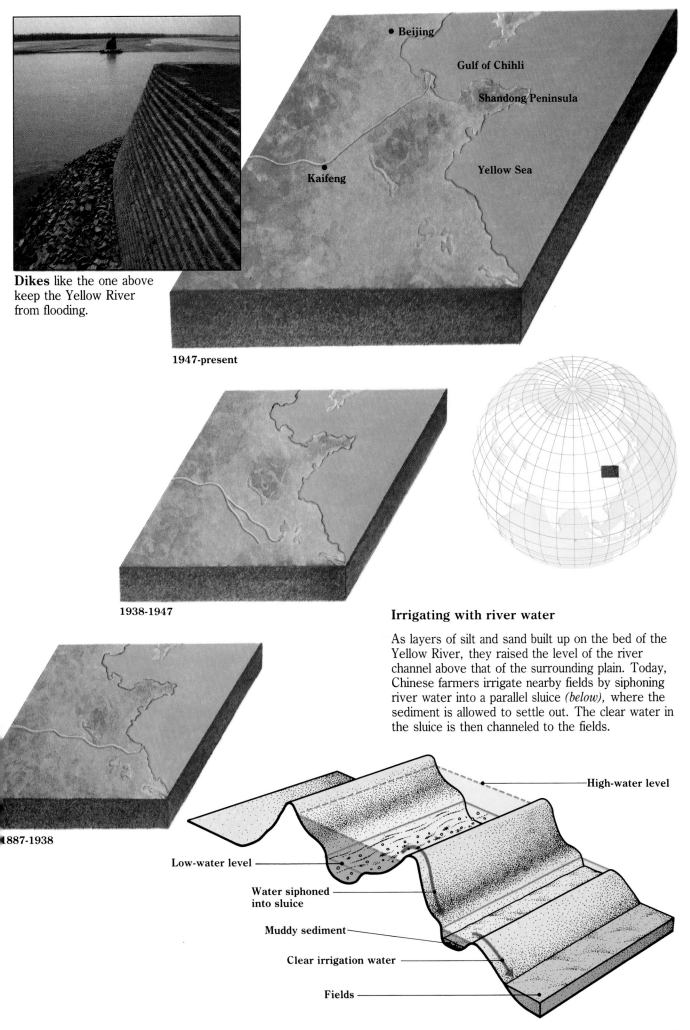

Dikes like the one above keep the Yellow River from flooding.

Beijing

Gulf of Chihli

Shandong Peninsula

Yellow Sea

Kaifeng

1947-present

1938-1947

1887-1938

Irrigating with river water

As layers of silt and sand built up on the bed of the Yellow River, they raised the level of the river channel above that of the surrounding plain. Today, Chinese farmers irrigate nearby fields by siphoning river water into a parallel sluice *(below),* where the sediment is allowed to settle out. The clear water in the sluice is then channeled to the fields.

High-water level

Low-water level

Water siphoned into sluice

Muddy sediment

Clear irrigation water

Fields

Can Rivers Flow Backward?

Starting as a spring high in the Peruvian Andes *(below),* the Amazon River gathers the waters of more than a thousand tributaries on its eastward journey across South America. One-fifth of all the world's river water flows through the Amazon, which drains 2.3 million square miles of land and pours water into the Atlantic at the rate of 80 million gallons per second.

Despite its mighty volume, the Amazon is a slowly flowing river; along its middle and lower courses, the river channel descends a mere ⅛ inch per mile. This level bed, combined with the river's wide mouth, subjects the Amazon to the periodic influx of ocean tides. Under certain astronomical conditions *(right),* high ocean tides override the Amazon's current and push inland, temporarily reversing the river's flow as far as 500 miles upstream.

Known as the *pororoca,* this tidal flood gives 10,000-ton river steamers a free ride halfway from the coast to destinations such as Manaus, in central Brazil, which lies 900 miles inland.

The Amazon drainage basin

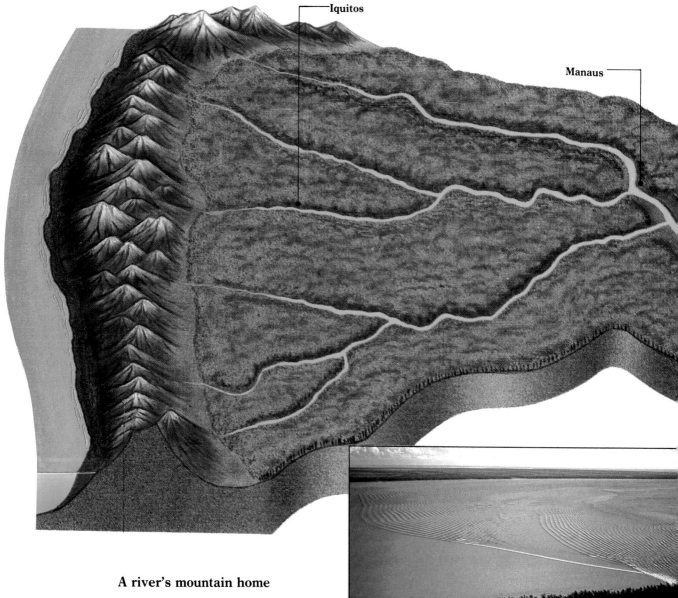

Iquitos

Manaus

A river's mountain home

Source of the Amazon and its tributaries, the Andes *(above)* run along South America's Pacific coast from Panama to Cape Horn. Stretching 4,500 miles, the Andes are Earth's longest mountain chain.

A ruffled flood tide swamps the Amazon, reversing its flow.

Why ocean tides occur

The tug of the moon's gravity on Earth lifts the water on Earth's near side, causing high tides. Gravitational force weakens with distance, so it pulls the water on Earth's far side only slightly. High tides still occur there, however, because gravitational forces drag the solid planet away from the overlying ocean *(below, left)*. Especially high tides take place during new and full moons, when the tidal forces of moon and sun align *(right)*.

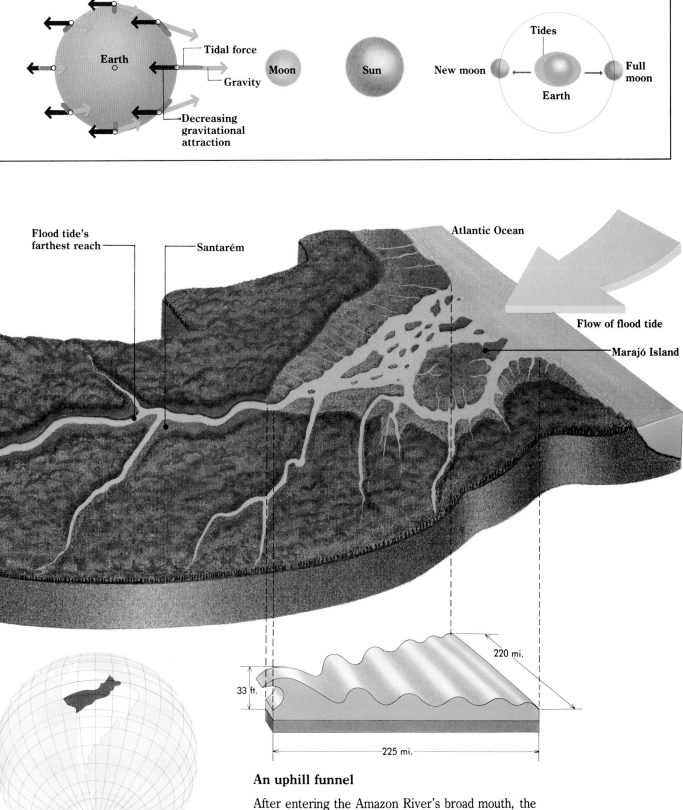

An uphill funnel

After entering the Amazon River's broad mouth, the flood tide advances upstream. Constricted by the narrowing river channel, the 7-foot tide gradually increases in height. By the time it has traveled 225 miles upriver, the surge—now a miniature tidal wave—measures 33 feet high.

What Are Estuaries?

England's Thames River empties into the North Sea through a broad, deep bay known as an estuary. Like many estuaries, this one formed at the end of the Pleistocene ice age some 10,000 years ago, when melting ice sheets raised sea levels worldwide. The rising ocean water submerged the river's mouth and lower channel, creating the estuary.

An estuary fed by a river carrying high volumes of silt may fill in and become a coastal plain. The Thames, however, is a mild-mannered watercourse that deposits little sediment at its mouth. As illustrated below, any debris that does build up is soon washed away by North Sea tides. Twice a day at high tide, a tongue of cold, dense salt water licks its way into the estuary, flowing along the bottom. Shooting seaward on top, meanwhile, is a layer of warm, buoyant river water. Friction between these two currents creates a turbulent middle layer of water that loops out to sea, carrying any accumulated sediment with it.

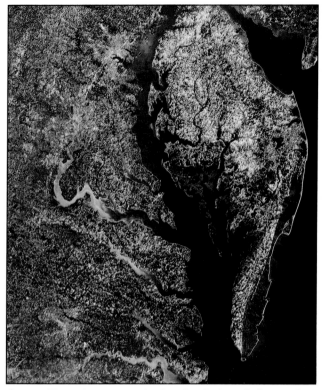

A satellite photo reveals the classic funnel shape of the Chesapeake Bay, one of the largest coastal plain estuaries in the world.

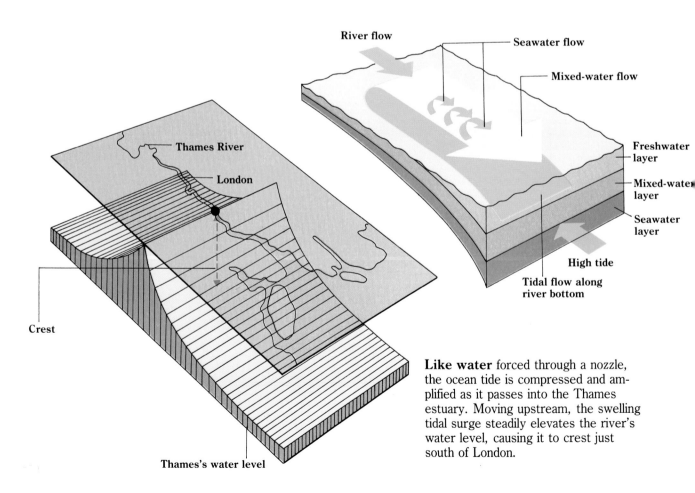

River flow

Seawater flow

Mixed-water flow

Freshwater layer

Mixed-water layer

Seawater layer

High tide

Tidal flow along river bottom

Thames River

London

Crest

Thames's water level

Like water forced through a nozzle, the ocean tide is compressed and amplified as it passes into the Thames estuary. Moving upstream, the swelling tidal surge steadily elevates the river's water level, causing it to crest just south of London.

An estuary often starts out as a delta *(left)*. Later on, as the sea level rises or the land surface sinks, ocean water engulfs the delta and the river valley behind it; this flooding creates the triangular bay known as an estuary *(below)*.

An estuary retains its conelike form only if tidal action regularly sweeps it free of channel-filling sediment.

39

Why Is the Rhine River Important?

High in the Swiss Alps, two mountain streams merge to form the Rhine River. From there the river flows north and west through the heartland of western Europe, defining portions of the national borders of Switzerland, Liechtenstein, Austria, France, and Germany. Along its middle and lower courses, the Rhine passes through the large industrial port cities of Mannheim, Cologne, and Duisburg in Germany. Finally, near the Dutch port of Rotterdam, it empties into the North Sea.

Linked by a web of rivers and canals *(right)* to ports in six different countries, the Rhine has become Europe's premier inland waterway. From the east, the Rhine receives the waters of the Main, Neckar, Ruhr, and Lippe rivers; from the west, it collects the waters of the Moselle. Canals connect the Rhine to the Rhone, Ems, Weser, Elbe, and Danube rivers—and, through these waterways, to the Mediterranean, the Baltic, and the Black seas.

The Rhine is open to ships of all nations. Vessels weighing up to 5,000 tons can venture as far upstream as Basel, Switzerland, carrying coal, ore, grain, and petroleum products. Larger ships have access to Duisburg, the gateway to Germany's industrial Ruhr Valley, where chemicals, iron, steel, and textiles are manufactured.

Barges ply the Rhine, a key waterway.

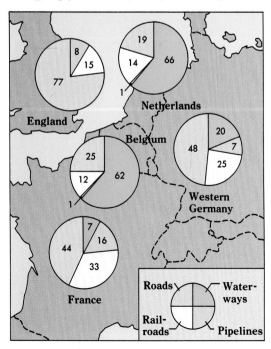

The up-and-down world of locks

Canal locks are special chambers that allow ships to navigate changes in elevation along a river's channel. Gates raise or lower the water level of a lock, floating a ship inside the lock to the next higher or lower level on the river's course. In the photo below, two ships pass each other in a lock on the Moselle River, which channels traffic between Germany and France.

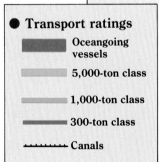

How Europe moves its cargo

Shipping goods by water remains the preferred method of cargo transport in Belgium and the Netherlands, where it accounts for nearly two-thirds of the total *(left)*. In western Germany and in France, trucks carry nearly half the goods, but cargo transport continues at high volume along the Rhine River.

● **Transport ratings**

— Oceangoing vessels
— 5,000-ton class
— 1,000-ton class
— 300-ton class
······· Canals

Europe's watery highways

North Sea

Kiel

Hamburg

Emden

Bremen

②

①

⑧

Amsterdam

Rotterdam

⑫ Netherlands

③

⑨

⑩

⑪ Dortmund

Duisburg

alais

Antwerp

Ghent

Brussels

Liège

Cologne

Bonn

Germany

Lille

Belgium

Koblenz

Luxembourg

Frankfurt

⑥

Mainz

Mannheim

Reims

Metz

aris

⑤

⑬

Nancy Strasbourg

Stuttgart

rance

⑭

Dijon

Basel

Switzerland

Liechtenstein

⑦

⑮

(1) Elbe River (2) Ems River (3) Rhine River (4) Seine
River (5) Marne River (6) Main River (7) Saône River
(8) Mittelland Canal (9) Dortmund-Ems Canal
(10) Lippe-Seiten Canal (11) Rhine-Herne Canal
(12) North-Holland Canal (13) Marne-Rhine Canal
(14) Rhone-Rhine Canal (15) Center Canal

How Do Glaciers Form?

When compressed, snow recrystallizes to form ice.

Glaciers are huge masses of ice that flow across the land like melted mountains. They form in alpine or polar regions, where permanent snow collects. As this snow builds up, it compacts the bottom layers into ice, and its weight causes the glacier to move. Most glaciers advance less than a foot a day, but some have moved 50 feet in 24 hours.

An alpine glacier is long and narrow; it inches down a ravine from a cirque—a bowl-shaped depression in the mountains. A continental ice sheet sits atop each of Earth's poles and on Greenland. And a piedmont glacier is a sloping ice sheet that spills from the highlands onto a low-lying plateau.

Glacial dynamics

In the accumulation zone, snow and ice accumulate faster than they melt. In the ablation zone, melting exceeds accumulation. Crevasses and fissures form when the glacier moves down abrupt steps in the underlying bedrock.

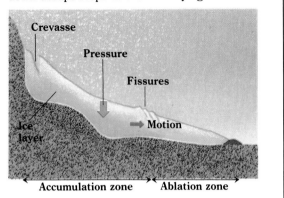

Crevasse

Pressure

Fissures

Ice layer

→ Motion

Accumulation zone | Ablation zone

1 Glaciers take shape in regions where snow accumulates faster than it melts. Fed by cold, moisture-laden winds *(blue arrow, right)*, a glacier amasses layers of snow that pack down to form ice.

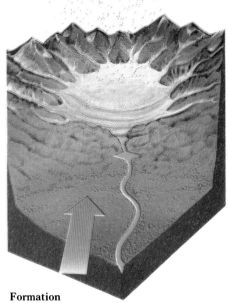

Formation

2 Subjected to the force of gravity operating on its own weight, the glacial ice eventually begins to flow downhill. If the glacier advances faster than it melts, it engulfs the valley below.

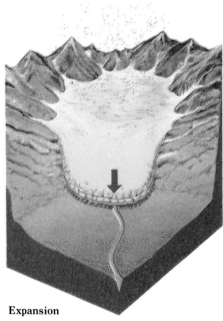

Expansion

3 In time, the rate at which the glacier is melting matches the rate at which it is moving downhill, and the icy giant seems to halt in its tracks. Although the glacier is in fact continuously flowing, its progress has been checked, so its terminus appears static.

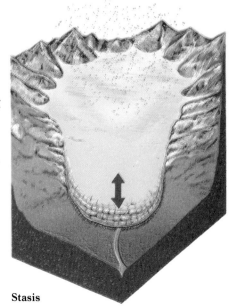

Stasis

Retreat

4 Tens or hundreds of thousands of years after the glacier formed, it begins to melt faster than it can move and begins to retreat up the valley.

What Landforms Do Glaciers Create?

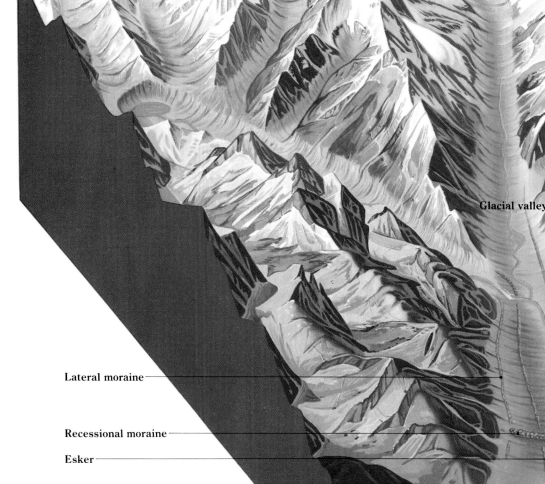

Horn

Glacial valley

Lateral moraine

Recessional moraine

Esker

A glacier is a natural bulldozer. Near the top of a mountain, it plucks blocks of rock from cliffs, hollowing out a bowl-shaped feature known as a cirque. Where three or more cirques intersect, spiky peaks called horns take shape. Downhill from these, the glacier gouges out a U-shaped trough as it grinds through an existing river valley.

The by-product of all this earth moving is enormous amounts of debris, which a glacier deposits as ridgelike mounds called moraines or oval piles known as drumlins. Eskers—narrow columns of sand and gravel— are laid down by streams of meltwater that have tunneled through the glacial ice.

How glacial landforms evolve

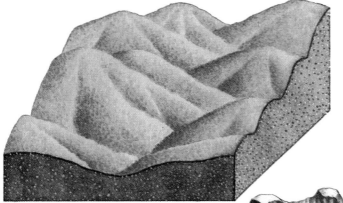

Before glaciation

A mountainous region, as yet untouched by glaciers, is covered with rolling slopes and V-shaped stream valleys. Such terrain results from gentle erosion by rivers, wind, and rain.

During glaciation

Sheathed in glacial ice, the same region exhibits knife-edged hollows where rounded mountains once stood. The glacier advances downslope, shaving away the rock in its path.

Cirque

Drumlin

Terminal moraine

After glaciation

Deep, U-shaped troughs testify to the passage of the glacier, now melted. At the mountaintop, jagged ridges and horns—more glacial handiwork—give rise to an alpine skyline.

A glacier's two-phase task

Alpine glaciers erode the underlying rock to create horns, cirques, and U-shaped troughs. Later, they redistribute leftover rubble in moraines, eskers, and drumlins.

A stream trips through a glacial trough in Austria's Alps.

45

Are All Moraines the Same?

Tons of fragmented rock, from particles of clay to boulders the size of a bus, are bound up in the flowing ice of a glacier. When the glacier retreats up a mountain valley, it sheds this rocky debris as moraines, or glacial deposits, of every shape and size.

Rubble carried on the underside of the glacier settles out as ground moraine, a rocky blanket that covers the land. Chunks of stone trapped between the glacier and the valley walls are deposited on either side in long ribbons known as lateral moraines. Frequently, a rocky trail called a medial moraine marks the center of the glacier's course through the valley; it formed when two smaller glaciers merged, dropping the rock that clung to their sides.

Stones and boulders pushed along at the glacier's front end collect in a curved ridge called a terminal moraine. This moraine marks the extent of the glacier's advance down the valley. Smaller recessional moraines show where the glacier stalled as it withdrew.

Ground moraine (1)—a mix of clay, sand, gravel, and boulders—is scattered over glaciated regions. While embedded in the glacier's base, the ground moraine scraped away the underlying surface layers and bedrock.

A recessional moraine (2) is a ridge of rubble unloaded by a glacier during a temporary halt in its retreat.

1   2

3

5

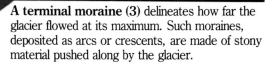

A terminal moraine (3) delineates how far the glacier flowed at its maximum. Such moraines, deposited as arcs or crescents, are made of stony material pushed along by the glacier.

A lateral moraine (4) consists of rocky debris the glacier scraped from the valley wall. Where two glaciers flow together, their lateral moraines merge to form a medial moraine (5).

How Were the Great Lakes Made?

Straddling the border between the United States and Canada is the world's largest system of freshwater lakes. These vast bodies of water, which are aptly titled the Great Lakes, were gouged out by a colossal ice sheet that once dominated much of North America.

About 250,000 years ago, the region now occupied by the Great Lakes was a low-lying plain. A continental ice sheet advanced into the area, digging depressions in the region's weak sediments. Successive glaciations—including one as recent as 30,000 years ago—deepened and enlarged these depressions. Some 14,000 years ago, as the ice sheet began to retreat, meltwater filled the hollows and created the forerunners of the Great Lakes. Geologic youngsters, the Great Lakes took on their present forms a mere 10,000 years ago.

13,000 years ago. In the vicinity of present-day Port Huron, the glaciers again advance, covering the predecessor of Lake Superior.

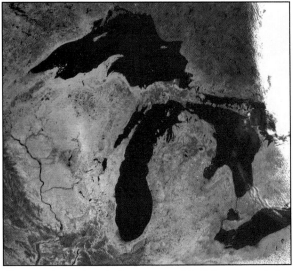

Scooped out by glaciers over a 30,000-year period, the Great Lakes cover 95,000 square miles today.

5,000 years ago. The glaciers have retreated completely, but the lake basins have not yet finished separating. Lake Michigan and Lake Huron, for example, form a single, interconnected body of water. Over the next 5,000 years or so, as the ice-free region rebounds, the current outlines of the Great Lakes take shape.

Lake Superior

Lake Michigan

Lake Huron

Lake Ontario

Lake Erie

14,000 years ago. The ice sheet recedes, creating short-lived lakes all along its front.

18,000 years ago. The glaciers reach their southern-most extent.

During a worldwide cooling trend some 30,000 years ago, the ice sheet that covered much of Canada began inching its way into the northern United States. Crushed by the weight of these glaciers, the region's lowland areas—including those that would become the Great Lakes—sank below sea level.

12,000 years ago. The ice sheet retreats, and the ancestors of today's Great Lakes form in its wake *(left)*.

11,000 years ago. The glaciers once more begin to move south, swallowing up the newborn lakes.

10,000 years ago. The glaciers begin a steady withdrawal, and the Great Lakes reappear.

How to make lakes

A glacier's weight depresses the continent below it, while its movement scours and erodes the Earth's surface. Then, as the glacier recedes, meltwater fills the sunken area, creating a lake.

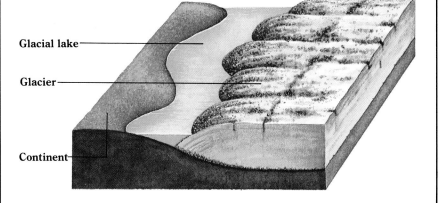

Glacial lake

Glacier

Continent

49

Did the Ice Ages Change Earth?

Throughout Earth's history, changes in the planet's path around the sun have triggered ice ages. In each ice age there were glaciations—periods when the ice sheets spread—and interglacials, or periods when the ice sheets receded. The most recent ice age, called the Pleistocene, comprised four major glaciations. Each one of these periods caused profound climate changes that led to worldwide shifts in sea level, vegetation zones, and topography (below).

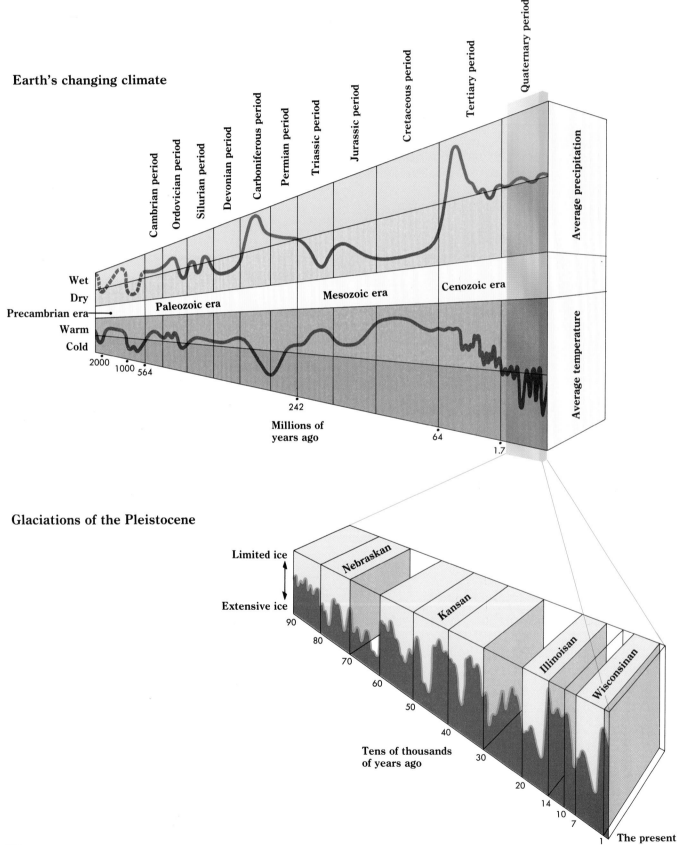

Earth's changing climate

Cambrian period
Ordovician period
Silurian period
Devonian period
Carboniferous period
Permian period
Triassic period
Jurassic period
Cretaceous period
Tertiary period
Quaternary period

Average precipitation

Wet
Dry

Precambrian era

Warm
Cold

Average temperature

Paleozoic era   Mesozoic era   Cenozoic era

2000 1000 564   242   64   1.7

Millions of years ago

Glaciations of the Pleistocene

Limited ice

Extensive ice

Nebraskan   Kansan   Illinoisan   Wisconsinan

90 80 70 60 50 40 30 20 14 10 7 1 The present

Tens of thousands of years ago

Ice-age makeover

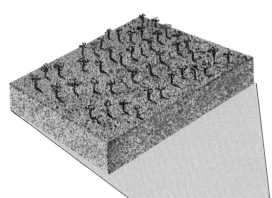

Northeastern Asia's Gobi Desert—largely a barren wasteland today *(right)*—was a tree-covered plateau *(left)* during the Wisconsinan glaciation 70,000 to 10,000 years ago.

The heart of the Gobi Desert is sand and gravel.

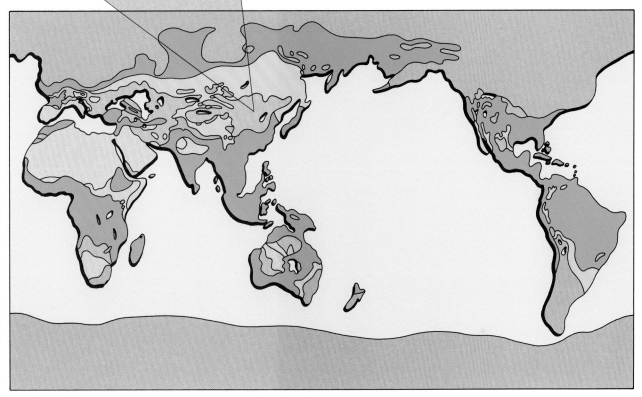

Changes wrought by ice

During Earth's last bout of worldwide glaciation, which ended some 10,000 years ago, the polar ice sheets expanded *(above):* In the Southern Hemisphere, glaciers reached as far north as Peru; in the Northern Hemisphere, they stretched into New Jersey.

	Ice sheet
	Arid (desert or tundra)
	Semiarid steppes
	Savanna or grassland
	Forest

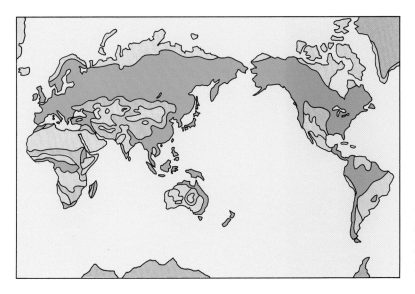

After the thaw

Since the ice sheets retreated, the temperate forests have reclaimed the higher latitudes, abandoning the middle latitudes to deserts and arid grasslands.

What's beneath Antarctica?

The continent of Antarctica is blanketed by 7 million cubic miles of ice. This icecap, which holds more than 50 percent of the world's fresh water, covers all but 1 percent of Antarctica. Only the continent's highest mountains pierce its icy shield.

These mountains, known as the Antarctic Transverse Range, divide Antarctica into two regions *(right)*. The larger, East Antarctica, embraces the heartland of the continent—a frigid, desolate plateau that lies buried beneath 9,000 to 10,000 feet of ice. West Antarctica, the smaller of the two regions, appears to be a solid landmass; in reality, however, it is a series of mountainous islands hidden under a mantle of ice up to 14,000 feet thick.

If the weight of Antarctica's icecap were removed, scientists speculate, the continent would rise as much as 2,600 feet. Parts of West Antarctica would remain below sea level, but other parts of the continent would ride as high as Asia. Given the region's climate, however, the ice is not likely to disappear anytime soon. In this polar land, where the sun remains below the horizon for months at a time, the daily temperature averages − 60° F.

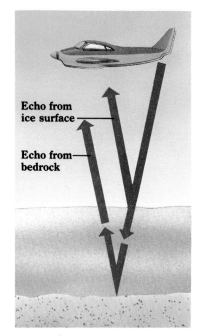

Echo from ice surface

Echo from bedrock

Seeing through the ice

In Antarctica scientists use radar to map the continent beneath the ice. Part of the radar beam reflects off the surface; the other part penetrates the ice and bounces off the bedrock. The time interval between the return of the two beams reveals the thickness of the ice and the contours of the land below.

Antarctic Peninsula

Antarctic Peninsula

Jagged mountains soar from the sea on the coast of Antarctica, Earth's coldest and highest continent. Inland, the mountains reach 16,000 feet.

Profile of a continent

Stripped of its icy cover *(above and below)*, only 60 percent of Antarctica would lie above sea level.

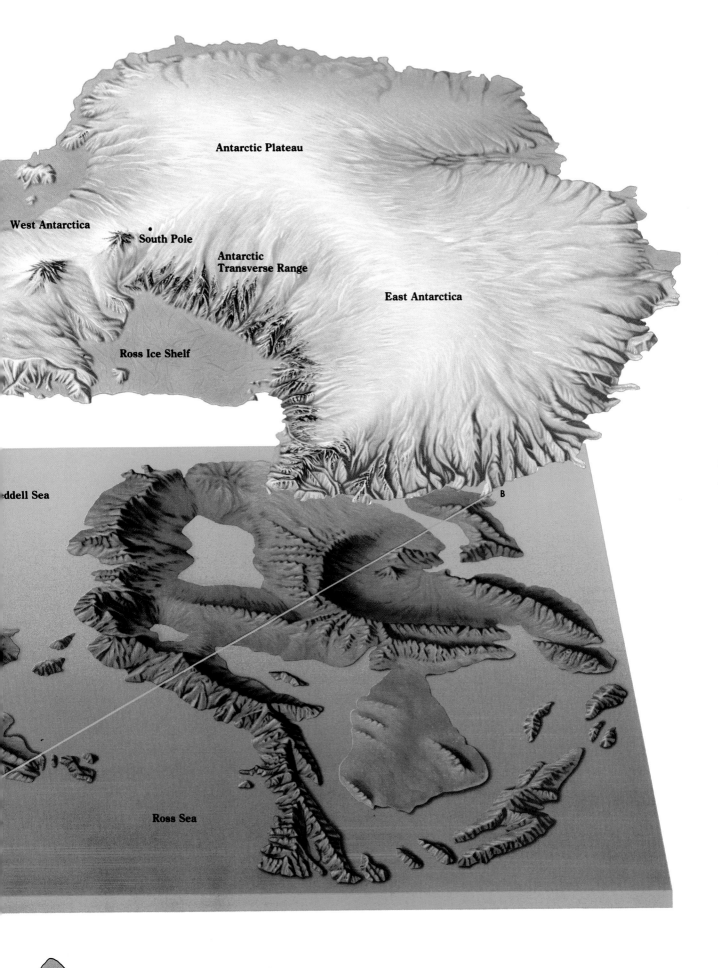

Antarctic Plateau

West Antarctica

• South Pole

Antarctic
Transverse Range

East Antarctica

Ross Ice Shelf

eddell Sea

B

Ross Sea

Antarctic
Transverse Range

Sea level

B

3

Ground Water and Lakes

Beneath Earth's surface, within the layers of soil and rock, lies a vast network of cracks, pores, and cavities filled with water. Much like the rivers and streams aboveground, this underground network forms an important part of the Earth's drainage system. Acting like a giant subterranean sponge, the underground system absorbs and slowly releases rainwater and snowmelt. Though hidden from sight, ground water is closely linked to life on the surface. Ground water provides a continuous source of water, even in dry months, as it seeps into rivers, lakes, and swamps, or bubbles forth as cold or hot springs. In the desert, ground water feeds an occasional oasis, making life possible in the most arid of climates. In regions where limestone rock predominates, ground water is a sculptor, dissolving the bedrock to form extensive caverns, sinkholes, and valleys.

For millennia, people have tapped ground water from springs and wells to use for needs ranging from drinking water to irrigation. But like other water sources, ground water can be easily polluted and may be overused. In many areas, chemical contaminants have seeped into the ground water supply, poisoning it. In other areas, pumping has exceeded the rate at which the water can be replenished. Consequently, the ground water supply has become seriously depleted. With a steady increase in world population, the demand for water continues to grow, and this resource must be protected from pollutants and overuse.

A world of unique beauty unfolds inside a dark limestone cavern, shaped by the relentless flow of ground water. Here, in Japan's Akiyoshi Cave, terraced pools called the Hundred Dishes seem to be sculpted from fluid stone.

What Makes Ground Water Flow?

Gravity drives the movement of ground water. As rain seeps into the soil, gravity pulls it downward until it reaches a level where water fills all the spaces in the soil and underlying rock. Once this area is filled, it is said to be fully saturated, and its upper surface is called the water table. In wet climates the water table may be only a few feet from the surface; in dry regions it can be hundreds of feet away. Gravity continues to act on ground water in the saturated zone, pulling it from places of high elevation, as under hills, to low-lying areas, as in valleys.

Any rock layer that holds water, yet allows it to flow, is called an aquifer. Not all rock strata allow water to run through; some are impermeable. When water seeping downward meets such a layer, the water may collect on top of the barrier, forming a zone of so-called perched ground water. Or an aquifer may be confined between two impermeable layers, allowing pressure to build in low sections of the aquifer because of the weight of the water above. Ground water always flows a little, averaging a speed between a fraction of an inch and several feet a day.

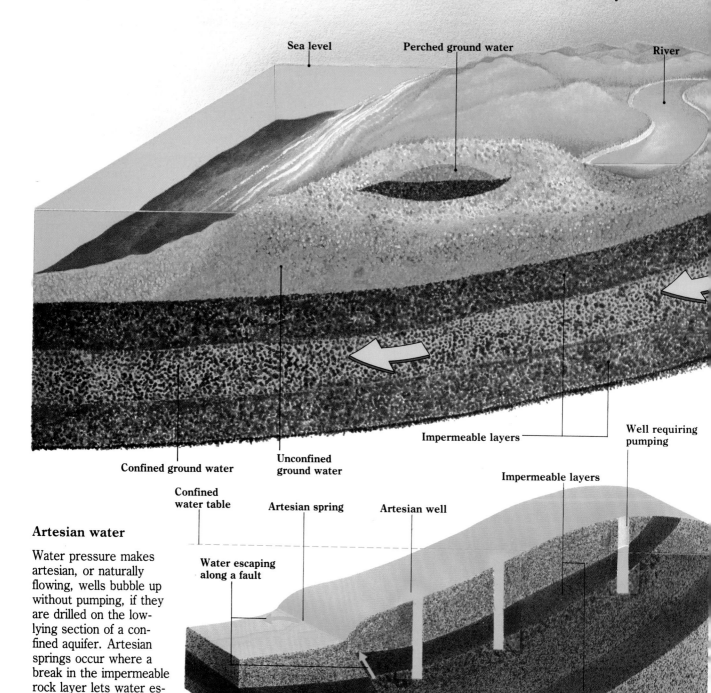

Sea level

Perched ground water

River

Confined ground water

Unconfined ground water

Impermeable layers

Well requiring pumping

Confined water table

Impermeable layers

Artesian spring

Artesian well

Artesian water

Water pressure makes artesian, or naturally flowing, wells bubble up without pumping, if they are drilled on the low-lying section of a confined aquifer. Artesian springs occur where a break in the impermeable rock layer lets water escape to the surface.

Water escaping along a fault

The flow of ground water

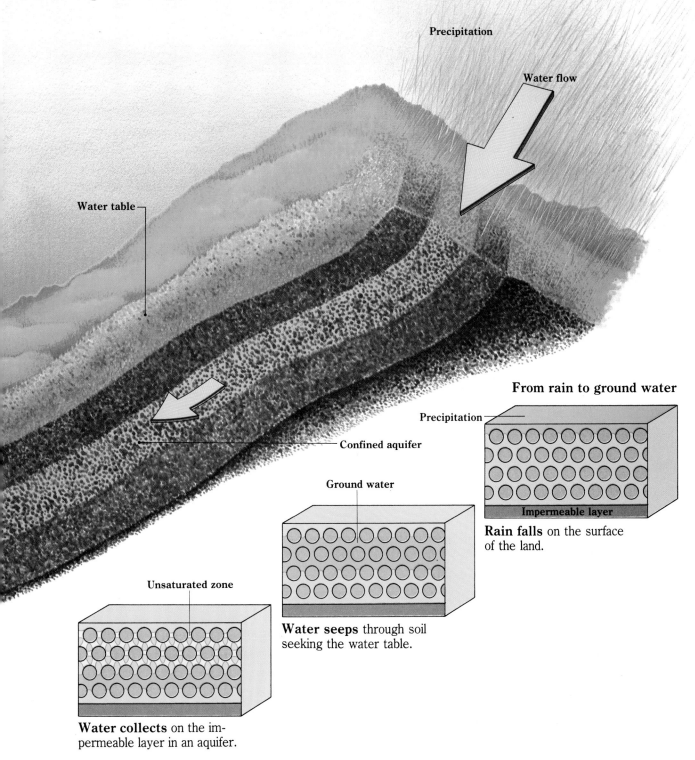

Precipitation

Water flow

Water table

Confined aquifer

From rain to ground water

Precipitation

Impermeable layer

Rain falls on the surface of the land.

Ground water

Water seeps through soil seeking the water table.

Unsaturated zone

Water collects on the impermeable layer in an aquifer.

Rivers and ground water

In dry regions, where the water table often lies deep in the earth, rivers and streams lose much of their water to feed the ground water system. By contrast, the water table in areas of high rainfall is often at or above the river level, so ground water feeds the river system.

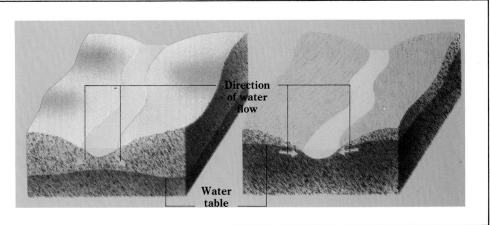

Direction of water flow

Water table

How Does Ground Water Shape the Land?

In terrain where limestone forms the bedrock, ground water can play a dominant role in shaping the landscape by dissolving the very rock it flows through. The movement of ground water is generally too slow to wear down rock the way a river erodes its banks. But when rainwater mixes with carbon dioxide from the air or the soil, it becomes naturally acidic and attacks and dissolves the limestone. At the surface, large troughs and sinkholes—pitlike depressions—appear where ground water has eaten away the rock below. Beneath the surface, ground water wears down joints and fractures, sculpting numerous caves. Where such features are common, the landscape is known as karst topography. Karst features develop slowly over thousands of years, forming best in warm, wet climates where ground water flow is plentiful. Despite abundant rains in karst regions, these terrains rarely support streams of any length. Instead, much of the rainfall quickly becomes ground water, often disappearing down sinkholes. In the United States, well-developed karst terrain can be found in several states, including Kentucky, Florida, and Indiana.

Erosion by ground water has etched a large karst plateau. Sinkholes and limestone outcrops give the land its gently rolling quality, while unseen caverns honeycomb the bedrock below.

Trough or karren

Flat-floored valley

3

Development of a karst plateau

In the initial stage *(right)*, ground water flows downward as well as crosswise through fractures and along rock joints, dissolving the limestone bedrock and creating long grooves or troughs called karrens. Small depressions begin to appear as sinkholes form.

1

Sinkhole

2

In the intermediate stage *(left)*, continued ground water movement widens existing flow channels, enlarging karrens into small surface valleys and shaping caverns below ground. Some caverns collapse, creating sinkholes in the ground above.

Merged sinkholes

China's tower karst

The tower karst of Guilin, China, represents a late stage in karst formation. These spires, formed between ancient sinkholes, are all that remains of a once-thick limestone layer.

In the mature stage *(left)*, smaller features continue to develop and combine. Sinkholes enlarge and merge, forming valleys. The cavern network expands but also collapses more frequently, helping to deepen surface features.

59

How Do Limestone Caverns Form?

Limestone caverns form in two distinct steps. In the first stage, the flow of slightly acidic ground water dissolves the limestone bedrock along seams and fractures. The water's flow carves the complex tunnels, passages, and rooms that form the cave itself. This takes place beneath the water table, so the cave passages are flooded during this process. Later, if the water table falls and the cavern drains, the second stage of cave development begins. Ground water seeping into the cave carries dissolved limestone from the bedrock above. As this mineral-rich water meets the air of the cave and begins to evaporate, it deposits its load of dissolved limestone, building an array of fantastic shapes drop by drop. Stalactites, stalagmites, draperies, columns, and terraced pools are just some of the formations that lend the cavern its eerie beauty.

Inside a limestone cavern

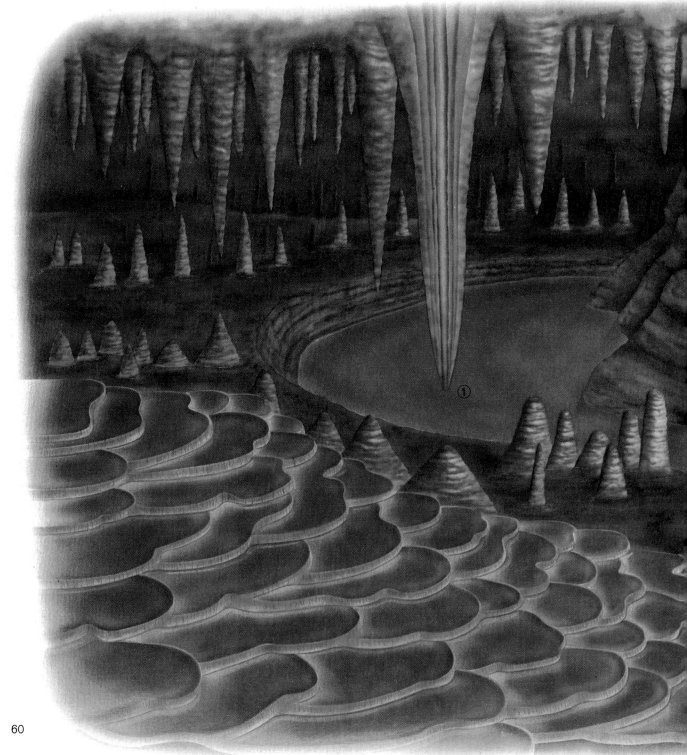

column forms where a stalactite and a stalagmite join.

Terraced pools form as water flows across a sloped surface.

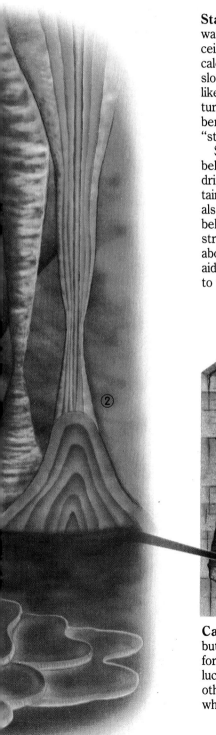

Stalactites (1) form where ground water drips through cracks in the cave ceiling. Each drop leaves a residue of calcite—dissolved limestone—that slowly accumulates, extending down like an icicle. Such structures take centuries to build. An easy way to remember stalactites is with the saying that "stalactites hold tight to the ceiling."

Stalagmites (2) rise from the floor below stalactites. Ground water that drips from the end of a stalactite contains enough dissolved limestone to also deposit calcite on the stalagmite below, adding with each drop to the structure until it joins the stalactite above, forming a column. A memory aid holds that "stalagmites might grow to the ceiling."

Drapery-shaped deposits

Cave formations vary not just in shape but also in color. Calcite, the mineral that forms most cave features, is usually translucent or milky white, but can be found in other shades—such as reds or grays—when mineral impurities are present.

61

Where Does an Oasis Get Its Water?

An oasis is a fertile spot in the desert where water is available year-round, often from springs whose source of ground water lies far from the oasis. The water that feeds an oasis usually originates in mountain regions, where, even in arid climates, some rains fall. Water entering an aquifer may emerge in a lowland oasis as an artesian spring, where a crack in the rock lets water surge to the surface.

Other aquifers appear on the desert surface in low-lying places where winds have scoured and eroded the land deeply enough to uncover the aquifer. Many oases, as in Africa's Sahara and China's Gobi Desert, draw their water from porous sandstone layers that begin in the mountains, which absorb the occasional rains. Rivers, such as Africa's mighty Nile, can also act as a source of oasis water. The water may be tapped at riverside or a long distance away through the water table. Whatever its source, oasis water is the key to survival for both humans and wildlife in harsh desert terrains.

The hidden source of an oasis

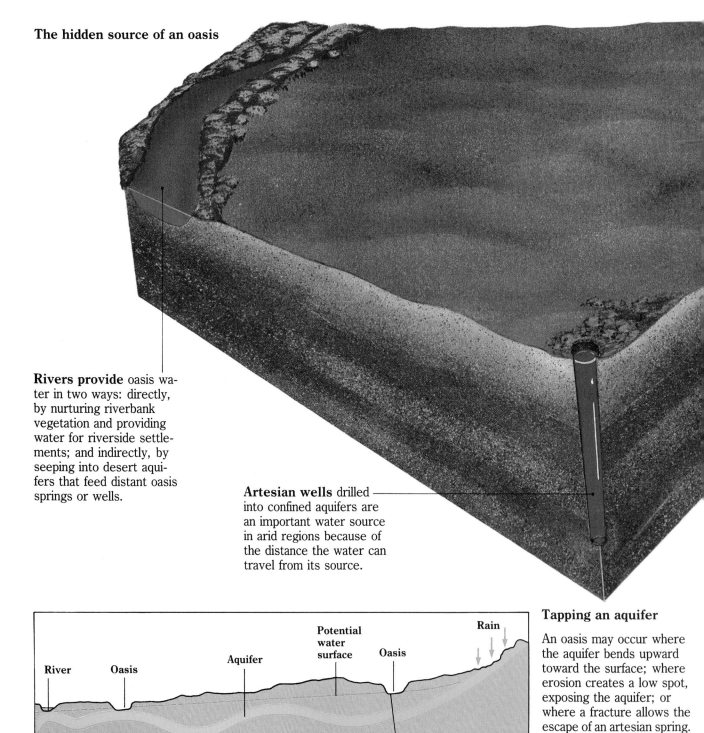

Rivers provide oasis water in two ways: directly, by nurturing riverbank vegetation and providing water for riverside settlements; and indirectly, by seeping into desert aquifers that feed distant oasis springs or wells.

Artesian wells drilled into confined aquifers are an important water source in arid regions because of the distance the water can travel from its source.

Tapping an aquifer

An oasis may occur where the aquifer bends upward toward the surface; where erosion creates a low spot, exposing the aquifer; or where a fracture allows the escape of an artesian spring.

An oasis in China's Gobi Desert supports a few plants.

An artesian spring may appear along a fault line when ground movement displaces the aquifer, interrupting its flow and leaving cracks so water can reach the surface.

— **Aquifers**

Marshes, springs, or lakes can develop where erosion cuts down to the aquifer level or where the aquifer tilts up, lifting the water table to the surface.

Rain

— **Shafts**

Design of a kanat

In some arid regions a special water system called a kanat is used to tap ground water from a hill and channel it to a nearby village without evaporation. A horizontal tunnel connects a source well to a collection channel at the base of the hill. A series of vertical shafts allows tunnel ventilation and maintenance.

What Causes the Ground to Settle?

Ground settling—known as subsidence—has many causes, but a common one is the excessive pumping of ground water from wells. Water that fills the pores of an aquifer helps keep these spaces from collapsing. Since water does not easily compress, ground water within the pore spaces can accept some of the weight from the ground above, helping the aquifer to maintain its structure. When this water is removed by pumping faster than the rate of normal water replenishment, the water table sinks and the water pressure in the aquifer falls. The reduced water level and pressure causes some of the pore spaces to compress, resulting in subsidence. If clay layers border the aquifer, subsidence may be particularly severe. As water pressure in the aquifer drops, the water in the clay layers is drawn out, and the layers compress. Overpumping of ground water can lead to other problems as well. Near the coast, reduced ground water pressure can allow salt water from the ocean to flow into the aquifer, contaminating coastal wells. Both subsidence and saltwater intrusion have become serious concerns in many coastal areas.

Subsidence damage

Subsidence can crumple foundations and paved streets; cause buildings to sink or tilt; break water and sewer lines; and ruin well casings and pumps, as shown below. Indirect damage includes flooding of subsided areas and the poisoning of wells caused by saltwater intrusion.

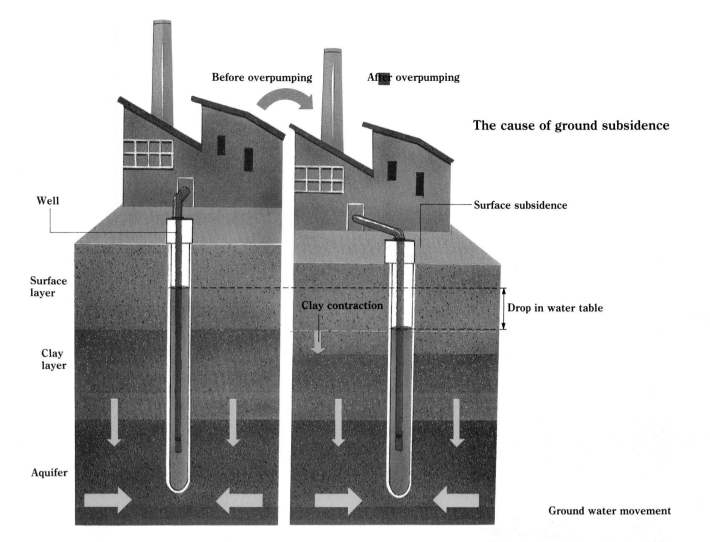

Before overpumping

After overpumping

The cause of ground subsidence

Well

Surface subsidence

Surface layer

Clay contraction

Drop in water table

Clay layer

Aquifer

Ground water movement

Cars and buildings are swallowed up by a 400-foot-wide subsidence pit *(left),* caused by heavy pumping of ground water *(shown schematically at top)* in Winter Park, Florida. Other subsidence problems can leave areas below sea level, as in the street in Tokyo shown above. Even when protected by levees or walls, such areas are subject to frequent flooding during severe weather, and drainage is always a problem.

Why Does Finland Have So Many Lakes?

Esker

Glacial rubble

Litorina Sea

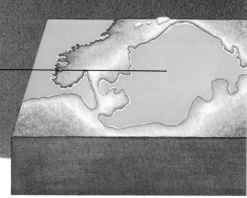

Ancylus Lake

4. About 7,800 years ago. The ice had melted, raising the water level again. A new connection with the Atlantic created the Litorina Sea, immediate predecessor of the Baltic.

3. About 9,500 years ago. Uplift formed a land bridge, turning Yoldia Sea into Ancylus Lake.

Some 188,000 lakes and ponds dot Finland *(shown in red on the globe at right),* covering nearly 10 percent of the total area. The flatness of the Finnish landscape and its poor drainage have left the water table high in most areas, allowing for the formation of a complex system of lakes and slow-moving rivers. Finland's soggy terrain dates from the melting of the continental ice sheet at the end of the last ice age. Most of the lakes fill shallow basins etched by the ice sheet as it advanced. Drainage was also influenced by masses of glacial rubble—sand, gravel, and boulders—left behind as the ice sheet retreated. In some places, this rubble is still visible as long, narrow chains of ridges called eskers, running north and south. Further complicating the region's poor drainage is the uplift that occurred when the weight of the ice sheet was removed. The uplift shifted drainage patterns and created vast swamps that hinder surface flow.

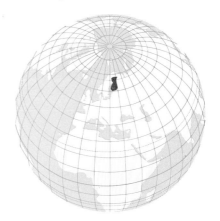

Formation of eskers

As the continental ice sheet retreated from the land that was to become Finland, meltwater formed vigorous streams flowing in tunnels within and at the base of the ice sheet. These streams transported tons of rock and debris scoured from the landscape. The debris settled in long ridge-like landforms called eskers that became visible when the ice sheet had melted.

Continental ice sheet

Baltic Ice Lake

1. Between 35,000 and 11,000 years ago. The continental ice sheet covering the Finnish region began to retreat, leaving behind the Baltic Ice Lake, a freshwater forerunner of the present-day Baltic Sea.

The evolution of Finland

Yoldia Sea

2. About 10,000 years ago. After further ice sheet melting, the Baltic Ice Lake rose and drained to sea level. Salt water, in turn, entered the lake, transforming it into the Yoldia Sea.

Lakes like this one dominate the Finnish landscape.

4
Oceans in Action

Powered by the rushing of the winds, the spinning of the planet, and differences in water temperature, Earth's oceans move in an endless rhythm. Ocean currents carry warm water from the equator toward the poles and cold water in the opposite direction. The coldest and deepest currents wind their way through a hidden landscape of towering mountains and abyssal depths at the bottom of the sea. Nearer the surface, warm, cleansing currents foster the growth of coral reefs throughout the tropics.

On a smaller scale, ocean waves and localized currents sculpt the planet in special ways. Where a sloping shelf of soft rock fringes the coast, for example, wave action eats away the land to form sea cliffs *(right)*. Swirling currents deposit the eroded debris as sand ridges and spits along the coast.

Still finer changes occur at the molecular level. Heated by the sun, the oceans transfer water to the air through evaporation. This process, part of the larger global water cycle, plays a key role in maintaining Earth's chemical and biological balance.

Along with rain, snow, glacial ice, and continental runoff, ocean evaporation dictates sea levels worldwide. The global effects of this and other ocean movements—including what would happen if the polar icecaps were suddenly to melt *(pages 72-73)*—are explored in this chapter.

Waves lap a beach in Normandy, France, where the advancing sea has chiseled the limestone shoreline into chalky cliffs and arches. The lone pillar at right shows where the coast once stood.

Is the Ocean in Motion?

Ocean currents act as global heat exchangers, moving water from the steamy equator to frigid polar waters and back again. On the surface of the sea, the currents are driven by major winds. Easterly trade winds push the water to the west, creating equatorial currents. Driven poleward by the Coriolis effect—a force arising from Earth's rotation—these currents merge with high-latitude currents to form grand circles, or gyres. The Coriolis effect steers gyres clockwise in the Northern Hemisphere and counterclockwise in the Southern Hemisphere.

Deep ocean currents are propelled not by wind but by differences in density. Cold, salty water is denser, or heavier, than warm, fresher water, so it tends to sink. The Antarctic bottom waters—the coldest on Earth—hug the seabed, where they creep toward the equator. Flowing from the opposite hemisphere are the slightly warmer waters of the Arctic, which ride above the Antarctic waters when the two meet. Where waters of different salinity collide, localized currents form. At Gibraltar, for instance, a salty tongue of Mediterranean seawater flows out into the ocean below a current of fresher Atlantic Ocean water moving in the opposite direction.

Water density and currents

Variations in seawater density drive the ocean's deep currents. The colder and saltier the water, the denser it is. Frigid polar waters migrate along the seafloor toward the equator.

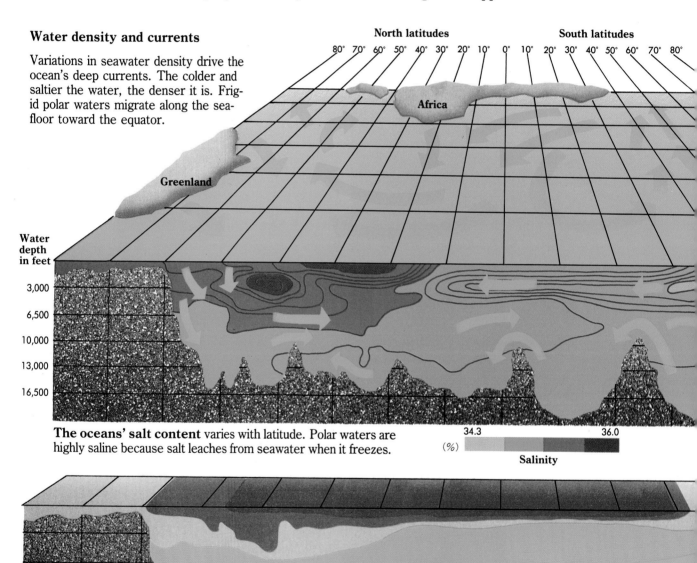

The oceans' salt content varies with latitude. Polar waters are highly saline because salt leaches from seawater when it freezes.

(%)   34.3   36.0
Salinity

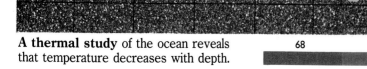

A thermal study of the ocean reveals that temperature decreases with depth.

68   59   50   41   37   32
Water temperature (° F.)

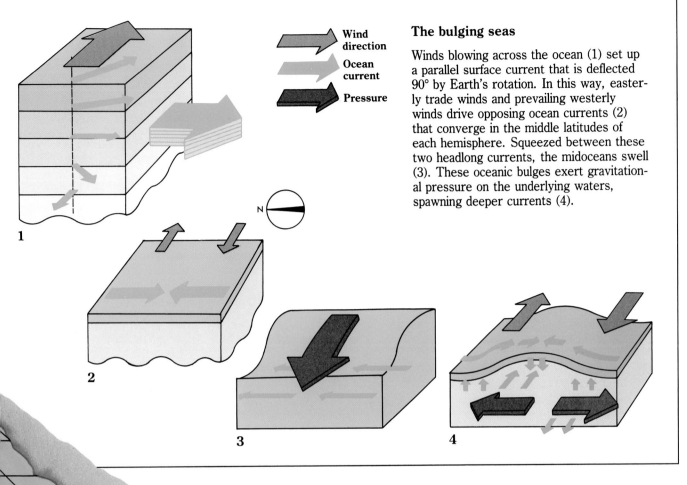

The bulging seas

Winds blowing across the ocean (1) set up a parallel surface current that is deflected 90° by Earth's rotation. In this way, easterly trade winds and prevailing westerly winds drive opposing ocean currents (2) that converge in the middle latitudes of each hemisphere. Squeezed between these two headlong currents, the midoceans swell (3). These oceanic bulges exert gravitational pressure on the underlying waters, spawning deeper currents (4).

Wind direction

Ocean current

Pressure

1

2

3

4

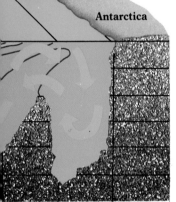

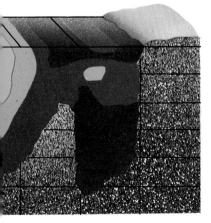

Antarctica

Forces shaping ocean currents

In each hemisphere, trade winds blowing from the east cause an ocean current to flow westward at about 15° latitude. Westerly winds, meanwhile, set a current flowing eastward at 45° latitude. The Earth's rotation, however, deflects each current from its straight-line course. Currents in the Northern Hemisphere therefore veer to their right, while those in the Southern Hemisphere veer to their left.

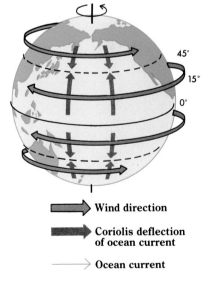

45°

15°

0°

Wind direction

Coriolis deflection of ocean current

Ocean current

World's widest whirlpool

The force of Earth's rotation bends a westward-flowing equatorial current poleward. At about 45° latitude it meets an eastward-flowing current, and the two merge to form a circular current, or gyre. Earth's spin pushes the center of the gyre toward the west, so the currents on the western side are narrower and faster.

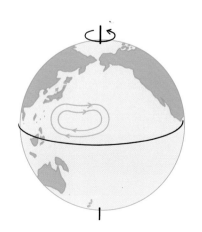

Could the Icecaps Melt?

The idea that Earth's polar icecaps might some-day melt is not as far-fetched as it sounds. At least three major ice ages have come and gone in the planet's 4.6-billion-year history. Some scientists believe that global warming, triggered by man-made carbon gases *(far right at bottom),* may slowly but steadily melt the icecaps that cover Greenland and Antarctica.

These two continental glaciers contain 99 percent of the world's ice. If they were to melt sud-denly, sea levels would surge worldwide. In order to estimate just how much the seas would rise, scientists divide the total volume of melt-water by the total area of the world's oceans. After accounting for the probable uplift of the ice-free Antarctic continent, they arrive at a global sea-level increase of 250 to 280 feet. This figure would diminish to approximately 150 feet over time, they speculate, as the ocean floor subsided under its weighty burden of water.

All but a few coastal buildings would be submerged if sea levels rose 250 to 280 feet.

Dunking the Big Apple

The skyscrapers of Manhattan would be engulfed by the sea if all the ice in Antarctica and Greenland suddenly melted. Sea levels around the world would rise as much as 280 feet. Eventually, as the sea-floor sank under the weight of the added water, the level would subside by 100 feet or so.

Manhattan as it looks today

The mechanics of melting

Carbon dioxide, produced by the burning of fossil fuels—gas, oil, and coal—admits light from the sun but keeps warming infrared rays from escaping into space. The buildup of greenhouse gases, as they are called, may raise global temperatures.

Sun

Visible light

Infrared rays

Manhattan as it would look if the seas rose 130 feet

Sinking the pyramids

Using the world's well-known structures as yardsticks shows how far above sea level the oceans would rise if the polar icecaps melted.

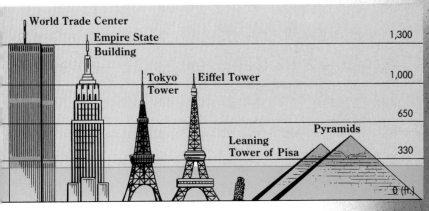

World Trade Center			
Empire State Building			1,300
Tokyo Tower	Eiffel Tower		1,000
			650
	Leaning Tower of Pisa	Pyramids	330
			0 (ft.)

How Do Sand Bars Form?

Constructing a sand ridge

Snagged by a coastal bay (1), a sand-laden ocean current reverses direction as it follows the contours of the shore. At the bay's mouth, the current deposits sediment that forms a sand bar (2). Over time, the sand bar stretches into a sand ridge (3); it may even enclose the bay to form a lagoon.

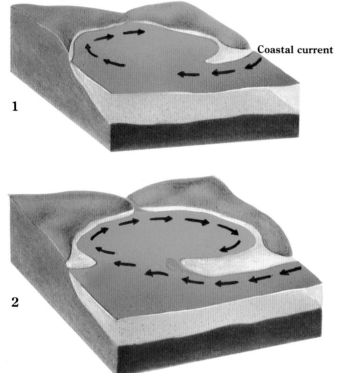

Coastal current

1

2

3

Curved at the end like a fishhook or tapering to a gentle point, a sand bar is the handiwork of ocean currents and waves. Through a process known as beach drift—caused by waves breaking at an angle to the shore—the currents pick up sand and gravel and carry them down the coast. Where an inlet or a bay channels these currents inshore, they strip even more sediment from the recessed shoreline and take it with them as they loop back out to sea. At the inlet's sheltered mouth, however, the wave action slows, causing the rebounding currents to dump their load of accumulated sand and gravel on the seabed.

Gradually, a mound of sediment called a shoal builds beneath the waves. In time—depending on the shape of the inlet, the strength and pattern of the ocean currents, and other variables—the shoal may rise above the water, forming either a sand ridge *(left)* or a sand spit *(right)*.

On occasion, a sand ridge may grow long enough that it forms a land bridge across the mouth of the inlet, blocking the ocean and transforming the recessed water into an isolated lagoon. If the lagoon is fed by a river, sediment will soon convert it into a marsh.

Scalloped with sandy beaches on its seaward side, this sand ridge has grown to span the mouth of a bay.

Cape Notsukezaki, on the Japanese island of Hokkaido, is a complex sand spit with a well-developed hook end.

Coastal current

Fashioning a sand spit

An ocean current swirls through a coastal inlet, stealing sand and gravel from the shore to build a sandy peninsula, or spit.

How Does the Sea Shape the Coast?

Wave-worn cliffs

Saw-toothed cliffs form along a coastline when ocean waves carve out pockets of weak rock, leaving recessed bays separated by capes of uneroded rock. Strong waves smash against the capes, then diffuse gently into the bays, where they build up sandy beaches.

Weak wave power

Strong wave power

Constantly in motion, the sea constantly batters the land. Where the coast is made of hard rock, the sea's destructive influence is slow and barely evident. But where a landmass is soft or shot through with weaker rock, the sea carves it into spectacular cliffs honeycombed with caves and buttressed by natural stone arches.

This sculpting action of the sea, known as marine erosion, works in three basic ways. The rhythmic pounding of the surf drives water into fractures in coastal rocks, widening the cracks. At the same time, sand and gravel suspended in seawater grind away at exposed rock surfaces. Finally, the seawater dissolves certain minerals in the rock and washes them away.

Subjected to this endless onslaught, the coastal rock gradually wears away and recedes. Sloping ledges erode and become steep sea cliffs, which in turn weather to form ragged capes and bays. Relentless waves then eat away at these toothlike capes, creating caves, arches, and even blowholes (*far right at bottom*). Ultimately, these too disappear, and only sea stacks—pillars of resistant rock—remain.

From cave to arch to column

Seawater carves a cave into each side of a protruding cape *(far left)*. Continuing wave action deepens the caves until they meet in the middle, forming an arch. Further erosion severs the arch at the top, forming a sea stack that will be consumed by the waves.

Marine erosion

Sea stacks and arches grace an ocean coast.

Benches by the sea

Hammering away at a landmass, ocean waves chisel a geologic formation that resembles a bench. The back of the bench is a sea cliff; the seat of the bench, which lengthens steadily, is an abrasion platform. Low tide *(above)* exposes the platform's planar surface.

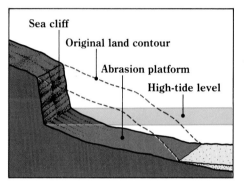

Sea cliff
Original land contour
Abrasion platform
High-tide level

Low tide reveals wave-cut benches near Iwaki, Japan.

There she blows!

Ocean water trapped in a cave at the base of a sea cliff may be expelled at high pressure by incoming waves. The opening through which the water escapes is known as a blowhole. Air released along with the water often makes a hissing sound.

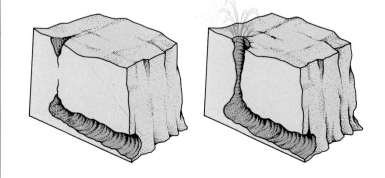

What Is the Ocean Floor Like?

Beneath the waters of the world's oceans lies a landscape of breathtaking extremes. The continental margins—which include continental shelves, slopes, and plunging abyssal trenches—form the boundary between the shore and the deep ocean basins. The basins are home to the mid-ocean ridge, a submarine mountain chain that rises as high as 2 miles above the seabed while meandering tens of thousands of miles around the globe.

Seafloor spreading—related to plate tectonics and continental drift—is responsible for the rugged topography of the ocean bottom. Molten rock oozes up through faults in the mid-ocean ridge, hardening into new seafloor material that shoves the existing ocean floor outward until it hits—and slides beneath—a continent or another seafloor plate *(pages 86-87)*. Ocean trenches, which mark this encounter, extend as deep as 7 miles below the surface of the sea.

The land beneath the waves

Like Earth's continental surface, the ocean floor is slashed by canyons and trenches, studded with towering mountains, and dominated by plateaus and low-lying basins.

A wealth of geologic features—from shelves and slopes to canyons and trenches—can be found along the continental margin, the transition zone from seacoast to seabed. Beyond the margin lies the rolling heartland of the ocean floor, where great plains and fractured plateaus fill the deep-sea basins. Flat-topped cones, called guyots, dot the basins.

Plateau

Continental slope

Channel

Continental shelf

Guyot

Ocean basin

Deep-sea trench

Trench

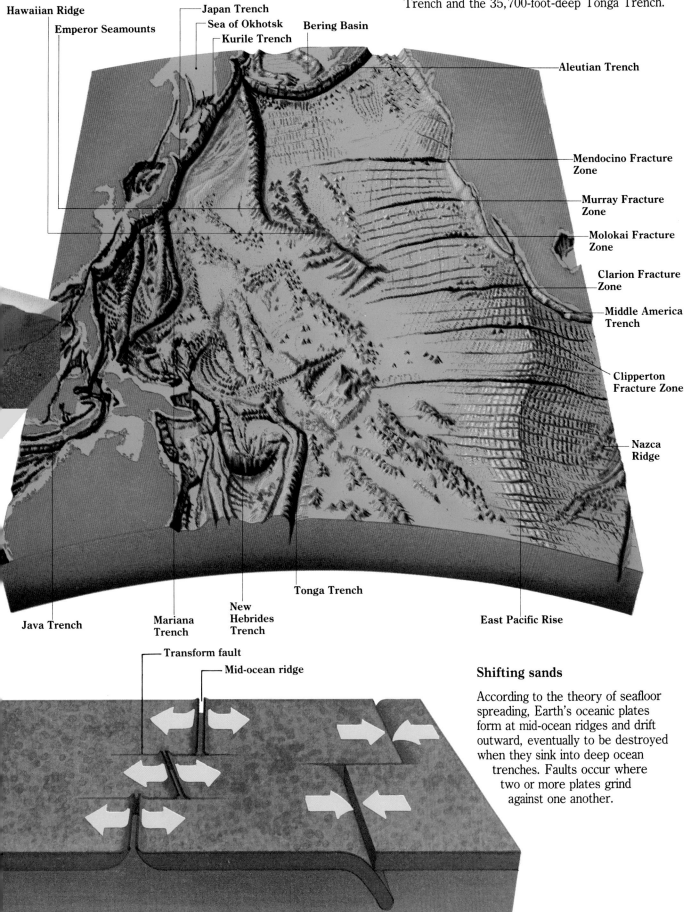

How low can you go?

Twenty-two of the oceans' 26 abyssal trenches rim the Pacific. The western Pacific harbors the two deepest, the 36,200-foot-deep Mariana Trench and the 35,700-foot-deep Tonga Trench.

Hawaiian Ridge

Emperor Seamounts

Japan Trench

Sea of Okhotsk

Kurile Trench

Bering Basin

Aleutian Trench

Mendocino Fracture Zone

Murray Fracture Zone

Molokai Fracture Zone

Clarion Fracture Zone

Middle America Trench

Clipperton Fracture Zone

Nazca Ridge

Java Trench

Mariana Trench

New Hebrides Trench

Tonga Trench

East Pacific Rise

Transform fault

Mid-ocean ridge

Shifting sands

According to the theory of seafloor spreading, Earth's oceanic plates form at mid-ocean ridges and drift outward, eventually to be destroyed when they sink into deep ocean trenches. Faults occur where two or more plates grind against one another.

How Do Coral Reefs Form?

As hard as rock and up to 60 miles across, a coral reef is home to millions of tiny tube-shaped animals, called polyps, encased in tough limestone skeletons.

Anchored to a rocky surface, a polyp catches plankton and minute shellfish with poisonous tentacles near its mouth. It also absorbs chemicals given off by algae living in its own tissues. These chemicals aid the polyp in secreting calcium carbonate, which hardens to form its body armor.

Cemented together in colonies, coral-reef polyps take on fantastic shapes ranging from lacy fans to brainlike boulders. They may be white, red, orange, yellow, purple, or other colors. A coral colony multiplies in two ways: by producing eggs and larvae, which develop into polyps, and by "budding," or sending out branching shoots of polyps. As shown here, massive coral colonies evolve to form fringing reefs *(right)*, barrier reefs *(below)*, or atolls *(opposite at bottom)*.

Coral's exclusive domain

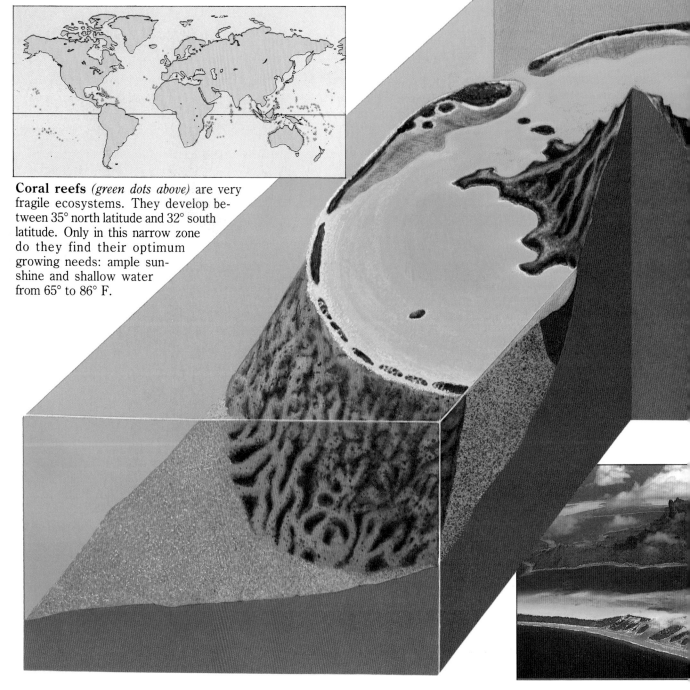

Coral reefs *(green dots above)* are very fragile ecosystems. They develop between 35° north latitude and 32° south latitude. Only in this narrow zone do they find their optimum growing needs: ample sunshine and shallow water from 65° to 86° F.

On the origin of reefs

In 1840 English naturalist Charles Darwin suggested an astute theory of coral-reef development. He identified three reef types—fringing, barrier, and atoll—and said they represent successive stages in reef growth caused by the sinking of the underlying landmass.

A fringing reef in the South Pacific

Building a fringing reef

A coral reef is born when free-swimming coral larvae migrate through the sea and attach themselves to rocks in the shallows of an island coast. Once anchored, the larvae grow into polyps. These adult animals then divide and branch out, building a dense reef that fringes the island.

A barrier reef

In the centuries following the growth of a fringing reef, the island begins to sink under its own weight. The reef continues to grow, building a barrier around the island. Water trapped between island and reef forms a lagoon.

A barrier reef protects Bora Bora.

A solitary ring

Eventually, the sinking island disappears, leaving the coral reef—now an atoll—encompassing the lagoon. A Pacific atoll and its lagoon are pictured at right.

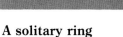

Why Don't the Oceans Overflow?

Every year, the Earth's oceans are flooded with approximately 100,000 cubic miles of water from rain, melting ice, and runoff from rivers. Despite this deluge, the seas remain at a constant level.

The reason lies in the world's water-circulation system, illustrated at right. Water is neither added to nor subtracted from the planet. Its abundance only seems to vary because it is in constant motion, cycling through the oceans, the air, the land, and back again.

The cycle begins as the sun evaporates water from oceans, lakes, rivers, and soil. Additional water vapor enters the air as plants extract water from the ground and release it through their leaves. The vapor then condenses as rain or snow, 75 percent of which falls on the oceans. Of the remainder, some evaporates; some pelts the land, rivers, and lakes; and some seeps into the earth as ground water, later to return to the sea.

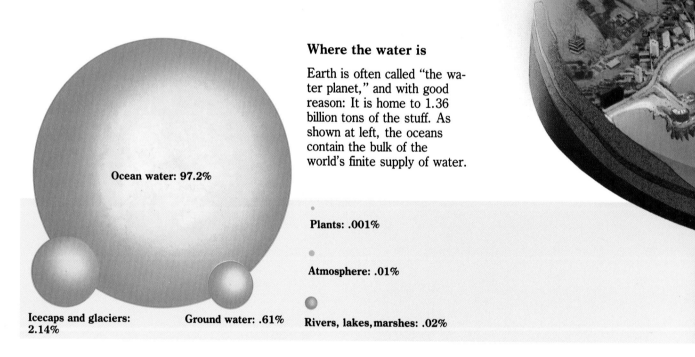

Where the water is

Earth is often called "the water planet," and with good reason: It is home to 1.36 billion tons of the stuff. As shown at left, the oceans contain the bulk of the world's finite supply of water.

Ocean water: 97.2%

Plants: .001%

Atmosphere: .01%

Icecaps and glaciers: 2.14%

Ground water: .61%

Rivers, lakes, marshes: .02%

Clocking the water shuffle

Though Earth's total volume of water never changes, the rate at which it cycles through the oceans, air, and land varies greatly. The chart below shows how many years it takes a hypothetical water molecule to work its way through a phase of the water cycle. Once a water molecule turns to vapor, for example, it stays in the atmosphere for about .025 year (nine days). But if it then becomes trapped in glacial ice, 10,000 years may pass before it moves on.

	0		0.2		0.4		0.6		0.8	1		10		100		1000	10000

Water vapor ‖ 0.025

Soil moisture 0.3 ~ 0.4

Glacial ice 10 ~ 10⁴

Ground water 10 ~ 10⁴

The global water cycle

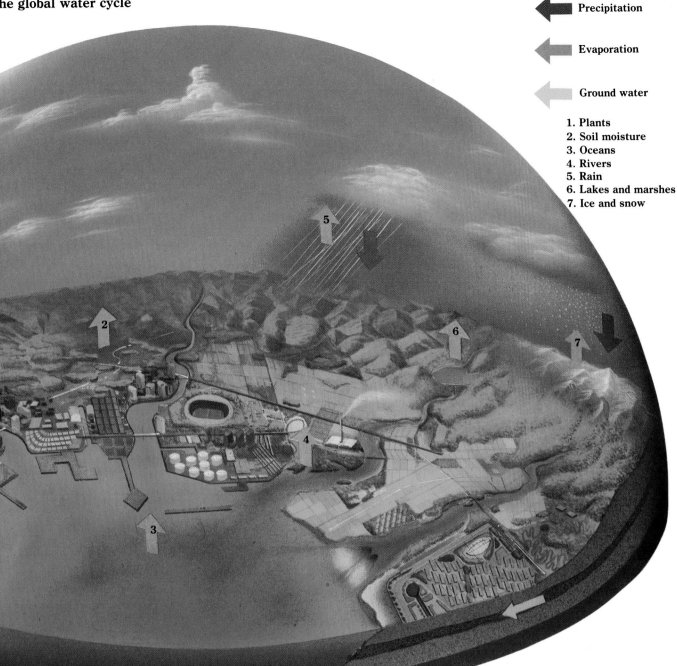

→ Precipitation

→ Evaporation

→ Ground water

1. Plants
2. Soil moisture
3. Oceans
4. Rivers
5. Rain
6. Lakes and marshes
7. Ice and snow

A fluid exchange rate

On a worldwide average, precipitation matches evaporation. From region to region, however, the exchange rate is uneven *(right)*. Over the subtropical oceans and the poles, evaporation exceeds precipitation *(far right);* the opposite is true over most high-latitude continents.

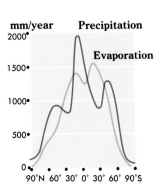

Precipitation exceeds evaporation

Evaporation exceeds precipitation

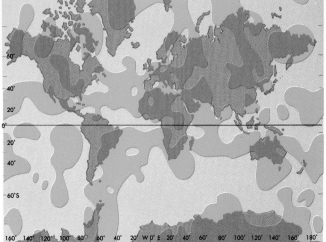

5
Molding the Face of a Planet

For all their seeming permanence, Earth's most monumental landforms—from the towering walls of Mount Everest to the spectacular terraces of the Grand Canyon *(right)*—are in a state of constant flux. Indeed, every part of the planet's surface changes every minute of every day.

The forces that cause these changes are many. They come from deep within the Earth, where heat and pressure raise and fold the planet's crust, causing the seas to rise and fall. They come from the atmosphere above the Earth, in the form of wind that gradually wears away even the hardest rock. And they come from the distant sun, which evaporates water from the Earth's surface. The water vapor then precipitates as rain or snow, forming streams that groove and channel their banks, rivers that cut through the highest mountains, oceans that engulf shores, and glaciers that grind hills into plains.

The transformation of the land has been going on for billions of years—that is, since the Earth first formed. As explained in this chapter, it will continue to occur as long as the planet exists.

The Colorado River has been scouring out the Grand Canyon *(right)* for the last 65 million years or so. The canyon will grow deeper and wider for millions of years to come—perhaps until the river reaches sea level, half a mile deeper.

How Are Mountains Formed?

Mountains rise above every continent and the floor of every ocean. The powerful forces that create them originate with plate tectonics—the grinding and bumping together of the rigid slabs of rock, called plates, that lie beneath the Earth's crust. Like flagstones riding on hot tar, the plates float over a layer of partly molten rock in the Earth's upper mantle. As the plates move, their outer edges frequently collide, pushing the crust upward to form mountains. This mountain-building process, known as orogeny, occurs in the three basic ways shown here.

Mountain chains result when two continental plates collide. The crust in the collision zone buckles and wrinkles, forming a chain of folded mountains like the Appalachians *(pages 96-97)*, the Alps, or the Himalayas *(pages 98-99)*. A mountain range like the Andes, which parallels the Pacific coast of South America, comes into being when an oceanic plate is driven beneath a continental plate. A third type of tectonic plate interaction occurs when an oceanic plate collides with—and is overridden by—another oceanic plate. This process gives rise to volcanic mountains, such as those in Japan and the Philippines.

The chiseled flanks of the Teton Range in Wyoming *(above)* are typical of fault-block mountains. The Tetons and other ranges of this type have sheer cliff faces on one side and gradual inclines on the other.

Fault-block mountains

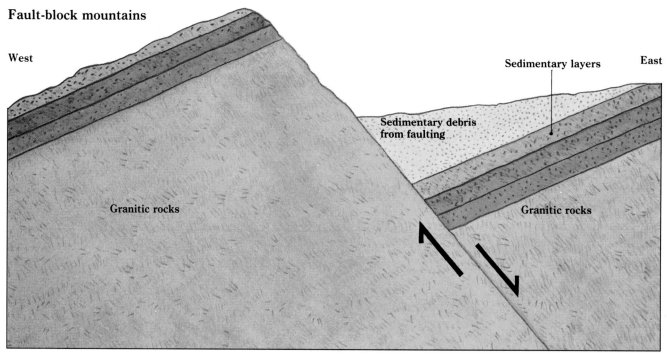

West

East

Sedimentary layers

Sedimentary debris from faulting

Granitic rocks

Granitic rocks

Located about 700 miles from the western edge of the United States, the Teton Range in western Wyoming *(diagram, above)* owes its existence to repeated movements of the earth along a steep fault that borders the range's eastern face. The crustal block on the east side of this fault has moved downward more than 10,000 feet with respect to the crustal block on the west side. The granitic rocks that make up most of the Tetons are covered by a veneer of sedimentary layers, which have been tilted westward by movements along the fault.

Mountains formed by colliding continents

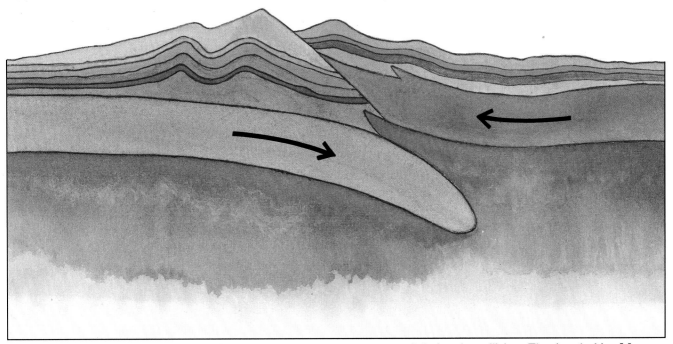

The collision of two continental plates that were once separated by an ocean produces folded mountain chains and large areas of regionally metamorphosed rocks—that is, rocks whose mineral composition has been altered by the intense pressures and high temperatures generated during the collision. The Appalachian Mountains were formed by just such a collision when the ancestor of the Atlantic Ocean closed up. After the collision and mountain building, seafloor spreading resumed and the present-day Atlantic slowly began to open.

Mountains formed by subduction

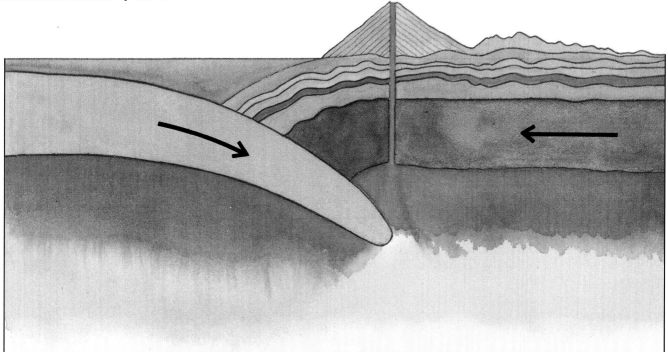

When an oceanic plate collides with a continental plate, the oceanic plate, being denser, is forced beneath the continental plate in a process known as subduction. The strong horizontal forces produced during this type of collision lift and fold the margin of the continent. As the subducted oceanic plate slips beneath the continental plate, it is forced to greater and greater depths; eventually, the oceanic plate melts along its leading edge. This molten material may then work its way up through the overlying continent and give rise to a chain of volcanoes, such as the Cascade Mountains. Mount Saint Helens is a subduction-related volcano.

How Are Terraces Created?

A river carries much more than water. Silt, sand, gravel, and clay, dislodged from the riverbed and banks by the force of the current, form a cargo of sediment that the flowing water transports downstream. As a change in climate or season causes the current to weaken, these river or stream sediments—known collectively as alluvium—are deposited and spread out beside the river. Then, when the current grows stronger again, the river cuts deeper into this alluvial material, dropping the riverbed to a lower level. The remainder of the flat-topped alluvium, one step above, becomes a river terrace.

Coastal terraces resemble river terraces but are formed by erosion, not deposition. When a drop in sea level exposes the sloping sea bottom close to a shore, the seabed becomes a coastal terrace. Ocean waves then smooth and flatten the terrace. If the waves batter the terrace where it joins the land, a steep sea cliff may form.

Carving a river terrace

A river erodes alluvium, or sediments, and carries it downstream. When the current weakens, the alluvium spreads out to form a wide, flat surface on either side of the river *(below)*.

As the river current regains strength—because of an uplift in the land, for example—its erosive power increases. The water carves a deeper channel, the riverbed drops lower, and the earlier alluvium becomes a terrace.

1

2

Making a coastal terrace

A drop in sea level causes the ocean bottom to emerge from the water as a coastal terrace. Waves chisel the edge of the new land, creating seaside cliffs.

When the sea level drops again—during a period of glaciation, for example—the newly exposed seabed forms a second, lower terrace.

1

2

Checkered by lush farmland, river terraces rise gradually on either side of the Katashina River in Japan.

The terraced coastline of Japan's Sado Island shows the eventual effect of a falling sea level.

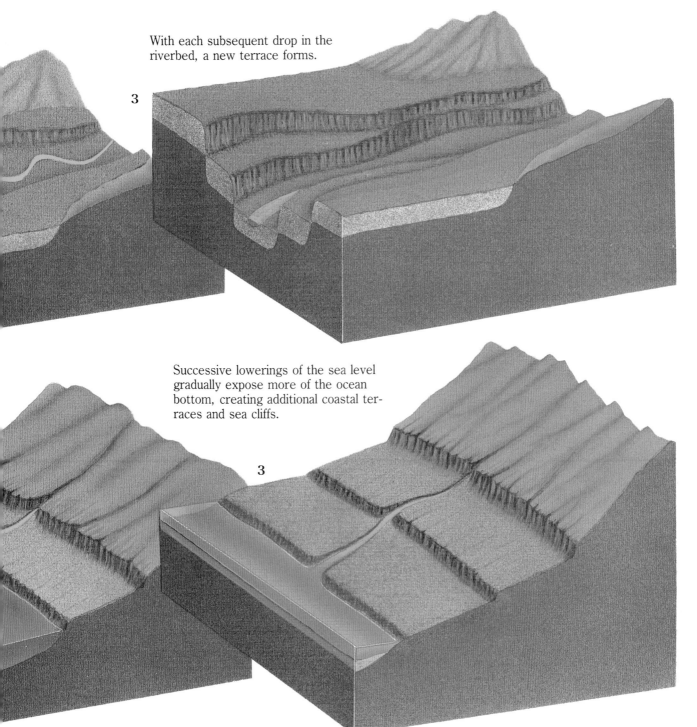

With each subsequent drop in the riverbed, a new terrace forms.

3

Successive lowerings of the sea level gradually expose more of the ocean bottom, creating additional coastal terraces and sea cliffs.

3

Can the Sea Invade the Land?

Sudden or gradual shifts in the Earth's crust or in the volume of the oceans can raise the sea level of a coastal area, allowing the ocean to inundate the land and form a new shore. The features of the remodeled coast—bays, inlets, peninsulas, or fjords—are determined by the shape of the land before the sea invaded it.

When the sea overruns an area of gently sloping hills, the result is drowned valleys; these are often dotted with islands and scalloped by inlets and bays, such as the Chesapeake Bay. A ria coastline, another type of drowned valley, takes shape when ocean water starts to submerge steep ridges that lie perpendicular to the shore. The ridges become fingerlike peninsulas and islands pointing out to sea, while the valleys are transformed into long, funnel-shaped inlets.

Where mountain ridges run parallel to the sea, ocean flooding produces a Dalmatian coast; as it has along Bosnia's seaboard, the rising water turns the valleys into sounds and the ridges into long, narrow islands. A fjord is born when the sea fills a U-shaped valley that was carved by glaciers.

This patchwork of inlets and islands is typical of a drowned valley.

A ria shoreline *(above)* is marked by deep, tapering inlets that alternate with long fingers of land.

How to drown a coast

A ria shoreline starts out as a seacoast whose steeply sloping ridges run perpendicular to the shore (1). As the sea level rises, the sea invades the valleys (2), forming deep inlets between narrow peninsulas and islands (3).

3

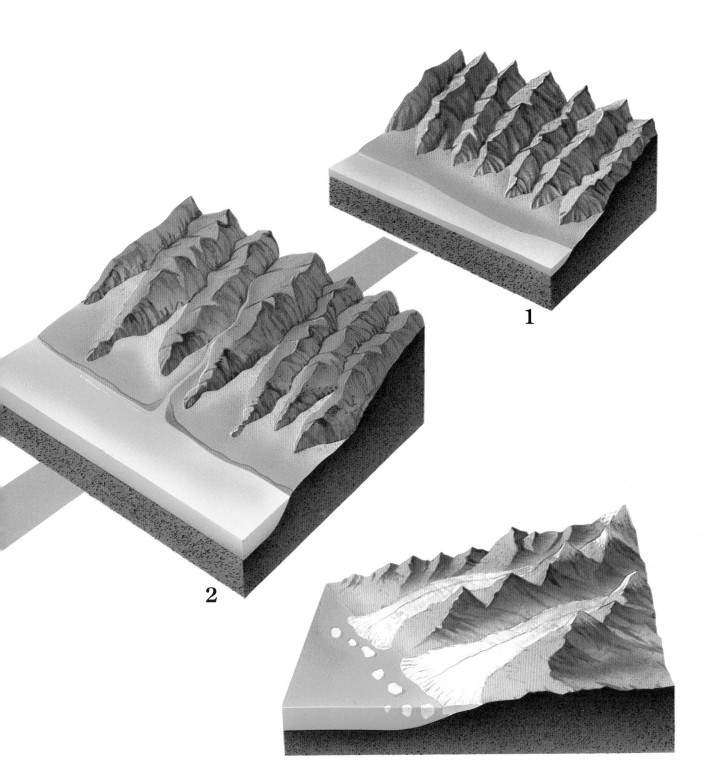

1

2

Forming a fjord

As glaciers slide to the sea, they gouge out U-shaped valleys with sheer, high sides *(above)*. If seawater later fills the valleys, it turns them into fjords.

Norway's serpentine coast

Fjords like the one at left abound along the crenelated coast of Norway. If every fjord in the country were stretched into a straight line, Norway's 1,238-mile coast would measure more than 8,000 miles.

91

What Is a Cuesta?

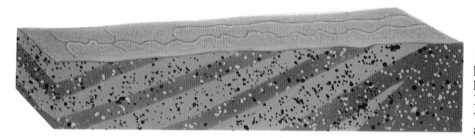

1. Shown at left is a slice of land likely to give rise to the low-lying ridges known as cuestas. Belowground, alternating bands of weak and resistant rock tilt at an angle of 15 degrees or less.

2. The weaker layers of rock—which may be clay or shale, for example—erode relatively quickly, leaving dips in the terrain. Resistant strata, such as limestone or sandstone, erode at a slower pace, forming gently rolling hills.

3. As wind and rain erode the land, the weaker strata wear down, leaving gentle slopes. The harder, more resistant strata remain in place, forming cuestas.

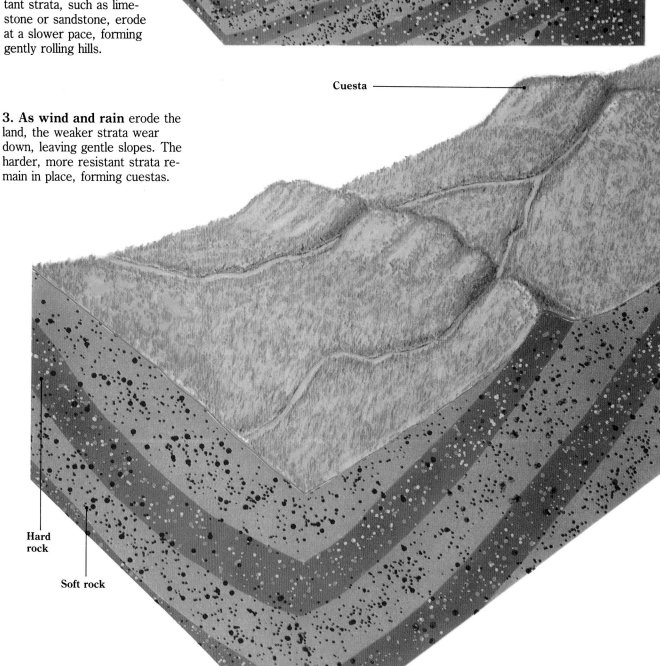

Cuesta

Hard rock

Soft rock

The contours of Earth's surface, like the contours of a sculpture, depend on both the forces that carve and the material that is carved. When the force is erosion and the material consists of gently tilted layers of sedimentary rock, the scene is set for the formation of long, low, parallel ridges called cuestas.

A cuesta has a distinctive profile. On one side is a steep face; on the other, a gradual slope. The ridge owes its shape to the alternating rock layers beneath it, which resist erosion with varying degrees of success. The cuesta itself is made of a hard, erosion-resistant rock layer. Sandwiching this stratum are softer layers of rock, which have eroded to form valleys between the ridges. Cuestas typify the landscape of the southwestern United States, the U.S. Atlantic and Gulf coasts, southeast England, and the Paris Basin.

Cuesta formations underlie rolling farmland in Normandy.

Cuestas in the Paris Basin

One of the largest cuesta formations is the Paris Basin, where alternating semicircles of hard and soft rock have left a pattern of concentric ridges and valleys. The center is the lowest point.

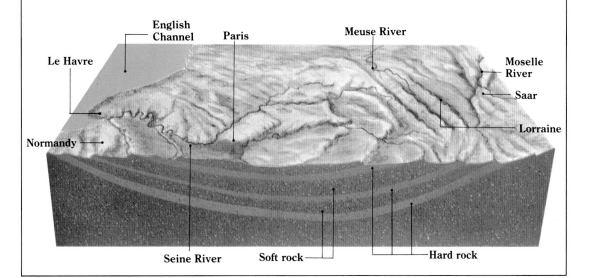

What Made the Grand Canyon?

Once upon a time—about 65 million years ago, in fact—the Grand Canyon was not so grand. In its place stood the Colorado Plateau, a 1.5-mile-high mesa that covered parts of present-day Colorado, Utah, Arizona, and New Mexico.

On that arid plain, the mighty Colorado River began its work. Through the corrosive force of water loaded with pebbles and sand, the river sliced its way down through the rock and created a canyon. Wind, rain, and snow then attacked the canyon walls, widening the gorge.

Today the Colorado Plateau and its magnificent Grand Canyon offer an at-a-glance review of Earth's geologic history. On the canyon walls can be seen the geologic evidence of volcanoes, deserts, dinosaurs, and ancient inland seas. The lowest exposed layer contains ancient igneous and metamorphic rock, some two billion years old, but no signs of life.

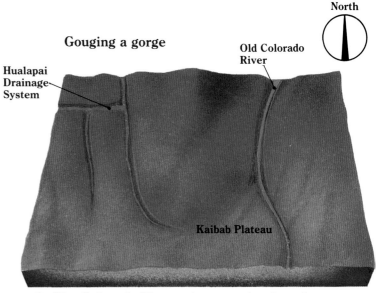

Gouging a gorge

1 **The Colorado Plateau** began to rise above its surroundings 65 million years ago. Before that time the area was at sea level, covered first by a desert and then, more than 250 million years ago, by a warm inland sea.

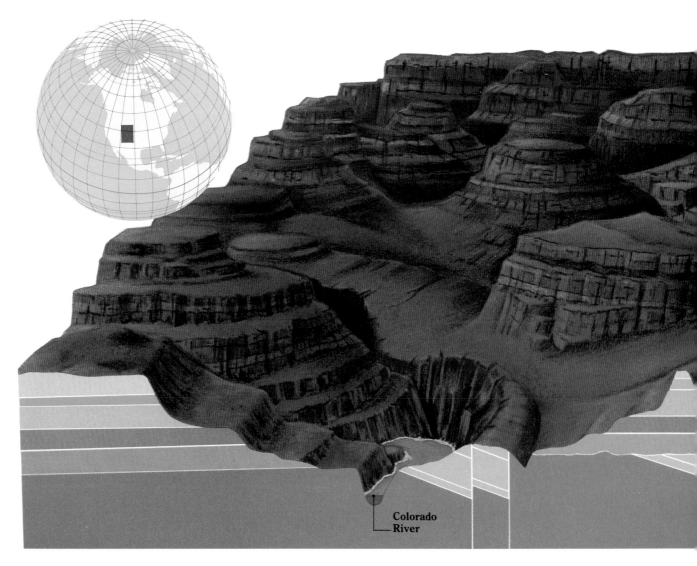

Colorado River

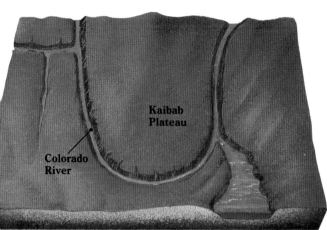

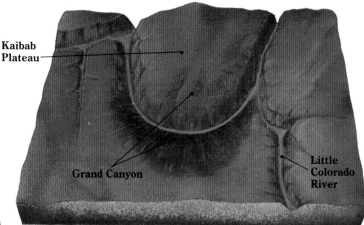

Kaibab
Plateau

Kaibab
Plateau

Grand Canyon

Little
Colorado
River

Colorado
River

3 **Assisted by** various agents of erosion—sun, wind, rain, snow, ice, and even the rock-shattering power of plant roots—the Colorado River took millions of years to carve the Grand Canyon.

2 **During the uplift** of the Colorado Plateau, the Colorado River was forced across the ~~K~~aibab Plateau. As a result, the watercourse joined ~~th~~e Hualapai Drainage System, creating the Colo~~ra~~do's present course.

Green with eroded sediments, the Colorado River gnaws away the floor of the Grand Canyon *(above)*. At right is a satellite view of the canyon area.

4 **Today the** Grand Canyon is 1 mile deep and up to 18 miles wide. Its layers of rock range in age from 250 million years at the top to two billion years at the bottom.

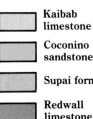

Kaibab
limestone

Coconino
sandstone

Supai formation

Redwall
limestone

Tonto group

Unkar group

Older igneous
and metamorphic
rocks

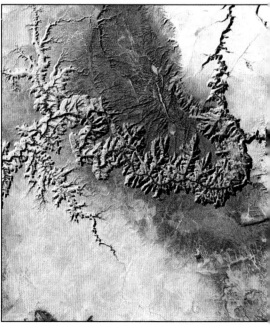

How Were the Appalachians Formed?

About 300 million years ago, a collision of continents—North America slowly slamming into Europe and then Africa—gave a tremendous boost to the Appalachian Mountains, which had begun to form some 200 million years earlier. The continental smash-ups generated intense heat and pressure, forcing a thick sequence of sedimentary rocks to rise up and fold Earth's surface into a mountain range tens of thousands of feet high.

Over the ensuing millennia, erosion, renewed uplifting, and more erosion shaped the Appalachians into their present form—a 1,600-mile-long range that stretches from Newfoundland through the eastern United States and into central Alabama. Today this mountain chain, one of the most extensively studied on the planet, boasts several geographically distinctive features, notably a network of limestone caves that honeycomb the ground beneath central and southern Appalachia. The tallest peak in the range is North Carolina's Mount Mitchell, which is 6,684 feet high.

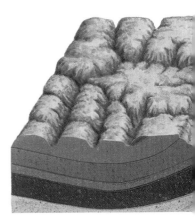

Deciduous trees blanket much of the Appalachian Mountains, creating autumn panoramas such as this one in North Carolina.

The biography of a mountain range

The Appalachian Mountains started to form some 500 million years ago. Continents parted, then drifted back to collide with one another, causing heat and pressure to build within the Earth. Eventually these collisional forces raised and crumpled the planet's crust into a mountain range similar to the modern-day Alps.

Continued erosion wore down the weak layers of rock but left the hard layers intact, exposing bedrock landforms that matched the original folds.

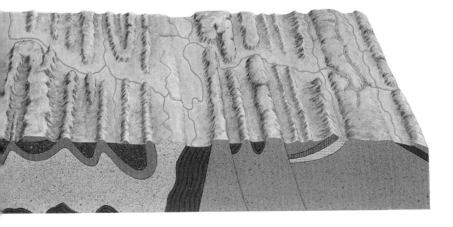

Today, the forces of erosion continue to grind away the Appalachian Mountains, softening ridges, smoothing out plateaus, and widening valleys.

Why Do Rivers Cross the Himalayas?

Some 40 to 60 million years ago, an ocean voyage ended with a bang when India, having migrated across the sea from Antarctica, crashed into the southern coast of Eurasia. Although the collision lasted millions of years, it occurred with such colossal force that it gave rise to the Himalayas, a mountain range with 30 peaks higher than 24,000 feet. Among them is the world's tallest, 29,028-foot Mount Everest.

Normally, mountains as big as the Himalayas would force rivers to flow parallel, not perpendicular, to them. But many of the region's oldest rivers—including the Indus, the Sutlej, and the Brahmaputra—were well established before the mountains began to rise. The upheaval was slow enough that the rivers continued to erode their courses as the uplift progressed; indeed, some of the rivers gained momentum as the mountains grew higher. In this way, the elevation of the ranges and the deepening of the river valleys took place in tandem, and the Himalayas came into being with a fully developed system of rivers that cross the mountains in deep gorges.

3 The rivers gained momentum as the mountains grew cutting deep gorges into the range.

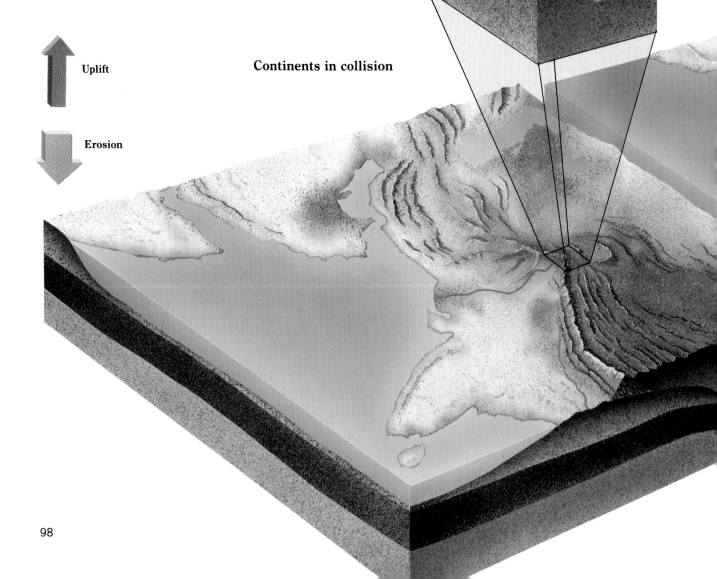

Uplift

Erosion

Continents in collision

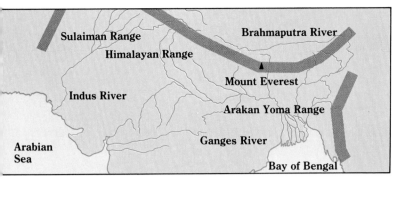

Map labels:

Sulaiman Range

Himalayan Range

Brahmaputra River

Mount Everest

Indus River

Arakan Yoma Range

Ganges River

Arabian Sea

Bay of Bengal

The Himalayas today

The Himalayas consist of several mountain chains. Two roughly parallel ranges embrace a 1,500-mile-long valley in which the Indus River flows east to west and the Brahmaputra flows west to east. A young system, the Himalayas rise an inch higher every five years.

1 **When India and** Asia collided, rivers already traversed the region.

2 **As the** mountains rose *(pink arrow),* the rivers kept pace, cutting valleys *(blue arrow)* into them.

Numerous river gorges cut through the Himalayas. The gorges range from 6 to 30 miles wide and from 5,000 to 16,000 feet deep.

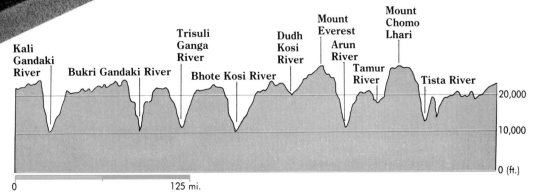

Kali Gandaki River

Bukri Gandaki River

Trisuli Ganga River

Bhote Kosi River

Dudh Kosi River

Mount Everest

Arun River

Tamur River

Mount Chomo Lhari

Tista River

20,000

10,000

0 (ft.)

0   125 mi.

6
Climate as a Force of Change

Set in motion by solar energy, wind and ocean currents crisscross the planet and shape its environment. To the tropics, they bring abundant rain and year-round warmth; to the poles, they bring endless winter. In the lands between these extremes, the currents create every type of climate from desert and forest to grassland and tundra.

Rainfall and temperature, the twin components of any climate, can dictate not only the vegetation but also the topography of an area. In well-watered mountain regions, for example, torrential downpours trigger landslides. And on a far longer time scale, freezing and melting water can split apart mighty boulders. Weathered by rain, the rock fragments then become grist for soil.

In regions without water, fluctuating temperatures and persistent winds combine to do the landscaping. Soft desert rocks, baked by day and chilled by night, crumble and are carried away as windblown sand. Resistant rocks yield more slowly to the desert winds, assuming fantastic shapes. Even the sand itself is molded by the wind into waving fields of dunes.

Climate—the agent of these environmental changes—is itself altered by the land and the sea. Mountains make winds shed their moisture, creating localized rain fronts. At sea, warm ocean currents relieve some of the chill from northern climes, while cold currents shuttle cooling relief to hot lands. Through this give-and-take, the planet and its climate create each other.

Shaped by the wind, these sand dunes in Egypt's Sahara are just one example of the climate's ability to transform the face of the land.

What Causes Landslides?

When heavy rains saturate the layers of soil and sediment on a steep mountainside, the water acts as a lubricant, causing the grains of earth to slide past one another and cascade downhill. These landslides, as they are commonly called, range in magnitude from minor rock slides that might block a road to catastrophic mudflows that can engulf whole towns.

Not every landslide, however, is triggered by water. A simple shift in the angle of a hill—brought on by an earth tremor or by human actions—can send surface materials careering downslope. Ground pitched at an angle of 25° to 40° is highly susceptible to this type of landslide.

Scientists classify landslides according to how they move. The most common type is creep—the very slow downslope movement of rock and soil under the influence of gravity. A free-falling shower of rock and debris is known as a fall. The gliding motion of a large slab of solid earth or rock that skids down a slope is referred to as a slide. If the sliding mass leaves a hollow in its wake, the landslide is termed a slump. The riverlike streaming of sediment and rock downhill is called a flow; this kind of landslide results when water invades soil or sediment.

The four stages of a slump

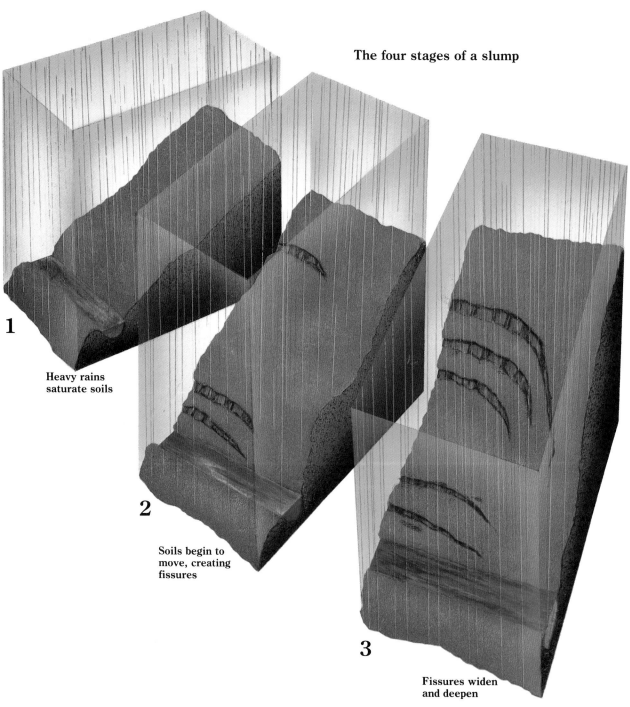

1

Heavy rains
saturate soils

2

Soils begin to
move, creating
fissures

3

Fissures widen
and deepen

Houses and other buildings lie buried beneath ~~ti~~ons of sandy soil from a landslide that rumbled ~~d~~own the face of Japan's Mount Jizuki in 1985.

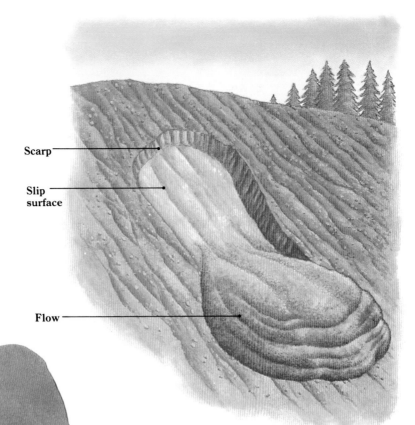

Scarp

Slip surface

Flow

When things go downhill

The landslide known as a slump is illustrated at left. Loosened by rain (steps 1-3), blocks of soil and rock slide downhill, creating new geographic features that range from flat toes and terraces to steep slip surfaces and scarps (step 4). Shown above is a flow, the downhill creep of water-drenched surface sediments. It can occur when topsoil thaws and slips away from the frozen layers beneath it, forming a slow-moving tongue of muddy debris.

~~Cu~~rved ~~sca~~rp

Slip surface

Fissure

Terrace

Original surface

Toe of slump

4 **Landslide occurs**

Can the Wind Create a Desert?

Earth's biggest deserts—the Sahara of Africa, the Rub'al-Khali of Saudi Arabia, and the Great Victorian Desert of Australia—are clustered in a relatively small area, the narrow band between 15° and 30° latitude in both the Northern and Southern hemispheres. These two zones are home to the trade winds—hot, dry air currents that circumnavigate the globe, driven by differences in temperature between the equator and the higher latitudes.

Air masses over the hot, humid tropics absorb moist, warm air and rise. As the hot air ascends, it cools and releases its moisture as rain *(box, right)*. The dry airstream then migrates toward the poles, growing colder and heavier until it sinks over the subtropical latitudes. Reheated during its descent, the air current—which is now called a trade wind—doubles back toward the equator; along the way, it blows across the continents as a hot, dry breeze. These parching winds have gradually transformed many subtropical lands into deserts.

■ **Rock + wind = sand**

2 At night, the temperature drops as much as 100° F., and the hot rocks cool and contract. This constant flexing weakens the rocks; buffeted by winds and windblown sand, the rocks fall to pieces over time.

1 According to one theory, desert sand is created by a process known as mechanical weathering. The process begins as searing daytime temperatures heat the desert rocks to more than 175° F., causing them to expand.

How winds make deserts

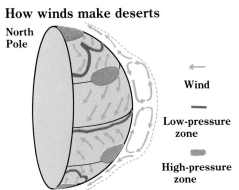

North Pole

→ Wind

— Low-pressure zone

▬ High-pressure zone

The sun's uneven heating of the atmosphere gives rise to winds that create high- and low-pressure zones.

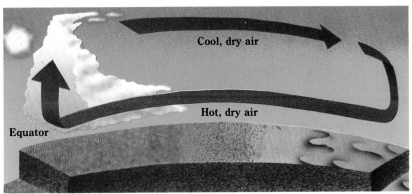

Cool, dry air

Hot, dry air

Equator

As heated air rises over the tropics, it cools and releases its moisture. Moving poleward, this air—now cool and dry—sinks and forms a sub-tropical high-pressure zone; out of this blow desert-making winds.

The sand dunes of the Sahara *(above)* may be the remains of rocks that were pulverized ages ago by heat and winds.

3 **Over eons,** desert winds scour the disintegrating rocks, carrying away fine particles of sand. These grains of sand slowly build up to form vast dunes.

Why Do Deserts Expand and Contract?

Scientists have discovered fossil evidence that many of the world's deserts were once lush gardens. The transition from paradise to wasteland may have occurred at the close of the last ice age, some 10,000 years ago. At that time, the polar icecaps began to melt. This caused the high-pressure zones—home of the hot, dry trade winds—to shift to higher latitudes *(globes, right)*, exposing large parts of the subtropics to these desert-making winds. The rains stopped, and fertile land turned to desert.

Today, desertification—the advance of the desert into nondesert areas—is being accelerated by human actions. A population explosion in the deserts' border regions has led to overgrazing of livestock, burning of forests to make fields, and overplanting. Stripped of its vegetation and nutrients, the soil erodes. To make matters worse, careless irrigation methods deplete the shallow reserves of ground water and encrust the earth with plant-killing salts.

These practices, compounded by drought, rapidly create deserts in already dry lands. Halting this trend will require major changes in human behavior—or, failing that, perhaps the onslaught of another ice age.

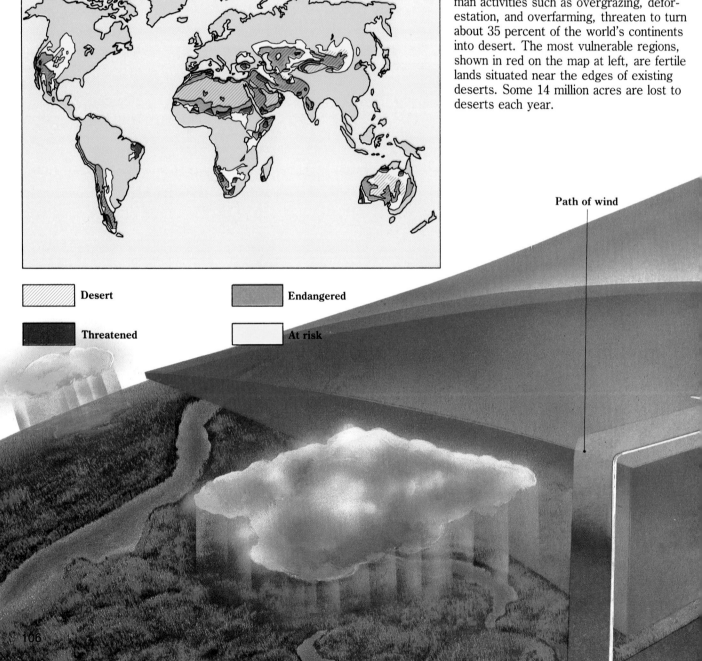

Desert | Endangered
Threatened | At risk

Path of wind

The march of the deserts

Natural climatic trends, combined with human activities such as overgrazing, deforestation, and overfarming, threaten to turn about 35 percent of the world's continents into desert. The most vulnerable regions, shown in red on the map at left, are fertile lands situated near the edges of existing deserts. Some 14 million acres are lost to deserts each year.

What's ice got to do with it?

When the icecaps spread during an ice age, the deserts shrink. The reason: The change in the planet's patterns of atmospheric heating narrows the trade-wind zones.

Trade-wind zones

During an interglacial period, the icecaps recede, so the desert-making trade winds flow from higher latitudes. Continental areas within these expanded trade-wind zones turn to desert.

Man's desert-making habits

Cattle forage on a denuded hill. Once a grassy range, the area was transformed into a desert by a mix of overgrazing and drought.

A farmer practices slash-and-burn agriculture, a leading cause of desertification.

How Are Dunes Formed?

Every dune forms around a "seed"—that is, a collection of pebbles, a shrub, or a slight irregularity in the surface of the desert. As the desert wind flows over and around this seed, it creates what is called a wind shadow on the far side. There, windblown grains of sand settle out and collect in a heap. The wind shadow of this tiny mound attracts more grains, and a sand dune begins to take shape.

Depending on wind speed and direction, the abundance of sand, and the lay of the desert, the growing dune eventually assumes one of the forms shown here. Most sand dunes have a gently sloping windward side, a steep, clifflike leeward side, and a knife-edged ridge in between. The wind rolls sand grains up the windward side to the ridge, where they balance until gravity propels them down the leeward slope. Whole dunes migrate across the desert this way, sometimes moving as much as 80 feet in a year.

Dune craft

Barchan dunes

A steady wind blowing across a level desert produces crescent-shaped barchan dunes *(left)*. The horns of each crescent point downwind; an angled wind may cause one horn to be longer than the other. The largest barchans measure 100 feet high and 1,000 feet across.

Barchanoid dunes

Secondary winds blowing at right angles to the prevailing wind sometimes sweep back the horns of barchan dunes, creating scalloped sand rows known as barchanoid dunes *(right)*.

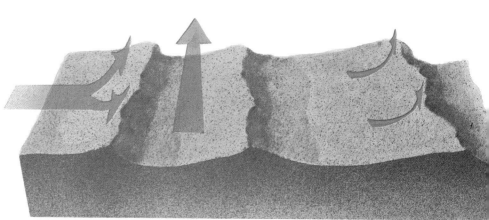

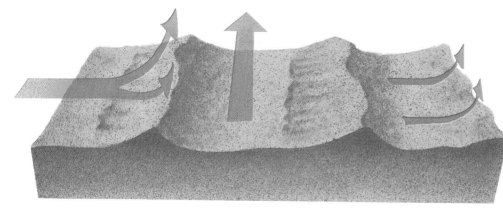

Transverse dunes

In regions where sand is plentiful, secondary winds streamline barchanoid dunes into transverse dunes *(left)*. Extensive plains of these straight-ridged formations are referred to as sand seas.

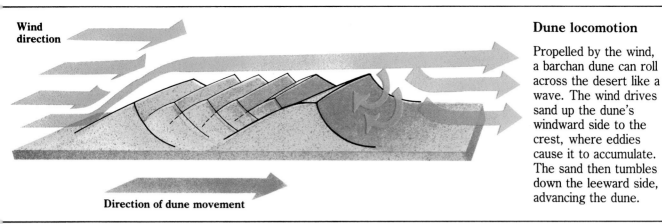

Wind direction

Direction of dune movement

Dune locomotion

Propelled by the wind, a barchan dune can roll across the desert like a wave. The wind drives sand up the dune's windward side to the crest, where eddies cause it to accumulate. The sand then tumbles down the leeward side, advancing the dune.

Star dunes

Sculpted by shifting winds, star dunes have multiple ridges arrayed like the points of a star around a high central peak. These isolated sand hills tower as much as 300 feet above the desert.

Longitudinal dunes

A strong wind blowing in one general direction creates longitudinal dunes that run parallel to the wind's course. Some are more than 60 miles long.

Dunes like the ones above fill much of the Sahara.

What Is Monument Valley?

At first glance, Monument Valley's curious monoliths—the rocky pillars that rise as high as 1,000 feet above the floor of the Arizona desert *(right)*—look like weathered mountains. In point of fact, however, they are the remnants of ancient plains. Once part of a flatland centered on the Colorado Plateau, the hard monoliths emerged as the soft sediments around them were stripped away by erosion.

The age and sedimentary content of the now-vanished plains can be read in the layers that make up a monolith. At the base is a skirt-like support made of 250-million-year-old sandstone and shale. Above the base, in the column-shaped center, lie the hardened remains of 245-million-year-old sand dunes that once blanketed the region. The youngest sediments—sandstones from 215 to 200 million years old—crown only the tallest monoliths.

The desert floor of Arizona's Monument Valley is hundreds of feet lower than the broad, flat plain that once covered its buttes *(above)*.

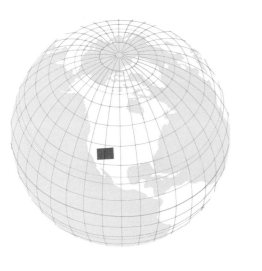

Rock-splitting rain

Carbon dioxide dissolved in rainwater forms a dilute acid that flushes minerals out of soft rock. Robbed of the elements that keep it intact, the rock crumbles.

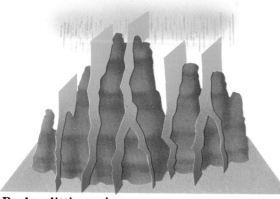

Making monuments

1 Some 65 million years ago, mountain-building forces began uplifting the Colorado Plateau, a level plain of ancient rock in the vicinity of modern-day Monument Valley. As the plateau rose, prehistoric rivers cut deep channels into its layers of sedimentary rock.

2 Over the centuries, chemical and mechanical weathering took its toll on the furrowed rock. The layers of stone were eaten away by acids in rainwater and shattered by ice that expanded as it froze in pores and crevices.

3 Winds laden with sand and dust, the by-products of erosion, constantly blasted the exposed rock layers, gradually wearing them away. Here and there, isolated columns of erosion-resistant red sandstone rose above the weathered plateau. As the winds continued their sculpting action, the columns were transformed into the towering needles, tablelike mesas, and trunk-shaped buttes that make up the "monuments" of Monument Valley.

Putting stones on a pedestal

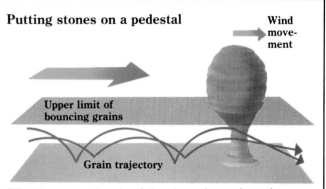

Wind-borne sand grains follow bouncing trajectories that carry them as high as three feet above the ground. The abrasive action of these grains cuts away the base of rock structures but leaves their tops intact.

Playing Rodin with rocks

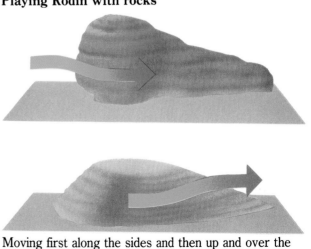

Moving first along the sides and then up and over the tops of rock masses, sand-laden winds chisel the stone into aerodynamic shapes known as yardangs.

Are Climate, Plants, and Soil Related?

Climate—how wet or dry, how hot or cold the weather is—governs the types and amount of vegetation worldwide. Indeed, scientists have outlined the main climate zones and their divisions largely by studying patterns of vegetation.

The average monthly precipitation and temperature for each zone are shown below. The zones correlate not only with vegetation zones around the world *(opposite page, top map)* but also with soil types *(opposite, bottom)*. Soil—made up of weathered rock and decayed plant matter—closely reflects climate. The reddish soil known as latosol is found in tropical rain forests, while desert or tundra soil is common in hot or cold dry regions with scrubby vegetation. The richest soils—black and chestnut—occur in temperate, semiarid zones where light rainfall does not flush away organic matter. Spodosol and brown forest soil develop in mild, humid climates.

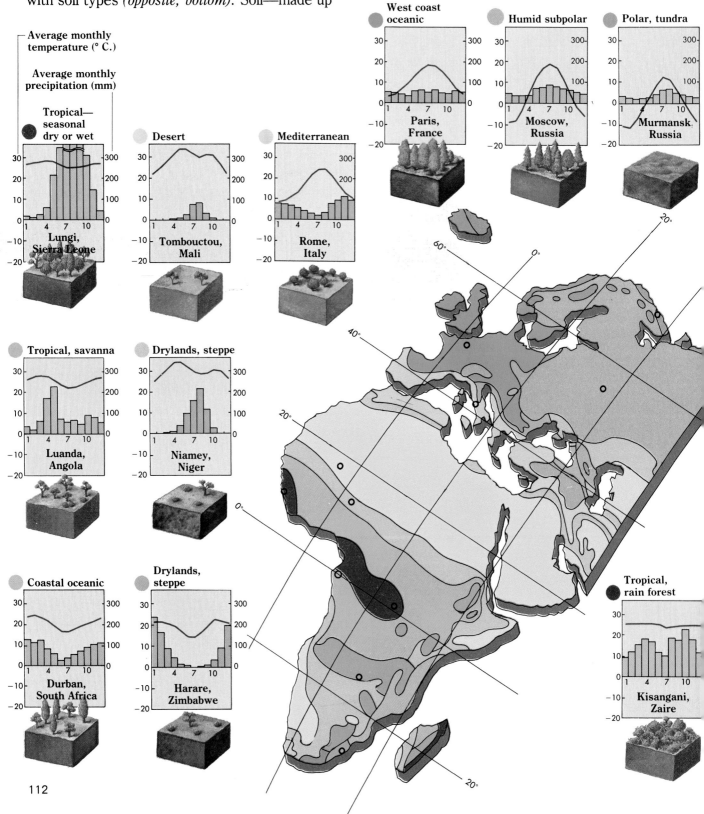

Vegetation zones

Temperature and rainfall regulate patterns of plant growth, so vegetation zones are keys to regional climate. A comparison of the maps on these pages reveals the relationship among climate, vegetation, and soil types.

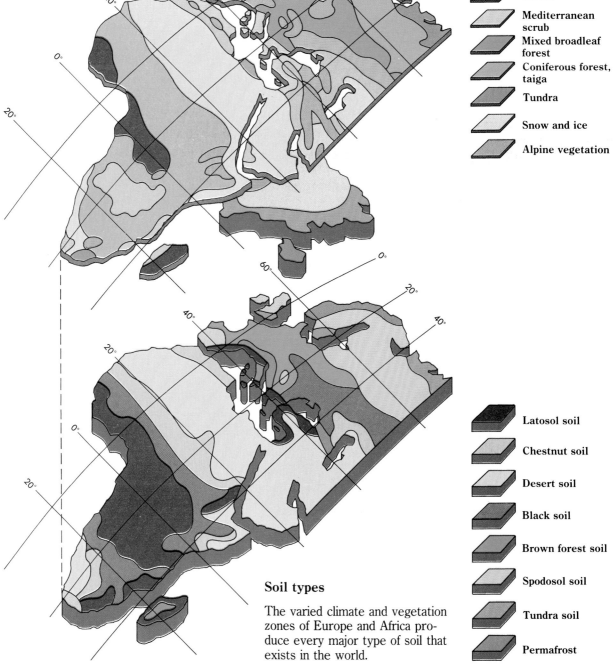

drought-resistant tree punctuates a patch of African grassland known as savanna. Semiarid savannas lie between deserts and rain forests.

- Tropical rain forest
- Subtropical deciduous forest
- Subtropical scrub
- Tropical savanna
- Prairie
- Steppe
- Desert
- Mediterranean scrub
- Mixed broadleaf forest
- Coniferous forest, taiga
- Tundra
- Snow and ice
- Alpine vegetation

- Latosol soil
- Chestnut soil
- Desert soil
- Black soil
- Brown forest soil
- Spodosol soil
- Tundra soil
- Permafrost

Soil types

The varied climate and vegetation zones of Europe and Africa produce every major type of soil that exists in the world.

113

Does the Land Affect Climate?

Heavy rains are the order of the day along the trade-wind coasts—that is, the eastern shorelines of continents located between the equator and 30° north or south latitude. The same is true for the western coasts of all landmasses swept by the prevailing westerly winds.

The reason lies in the interaction of air, sea, and land. As winds blow across the ocean, they sop up evaporated water. Later on, when these humid sea winds hit a continental coast, they rise and cool, causing their water to condense out as rain. If the coast is mountainous, the slopes make the winds rise and cool quickly, and the rainfall is even heavier.

Most of the precipitation occurs in a narrow belt along the coast or on the windward side of the mountains. Beyond this zone lies what is called the rain shadow—an arid region where the winds, which have been robbed of their moisture, shed little if any rain.

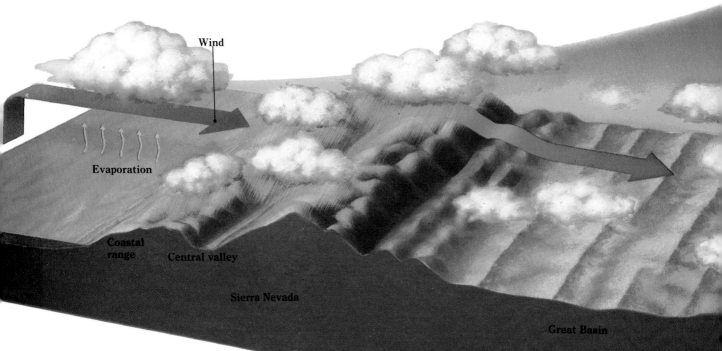

A checkered climate

Rain forests and deserts lie almost side by side in the western United States. Abrupt changes in land elevation can cause wide variations in climate *(maps, below)*.

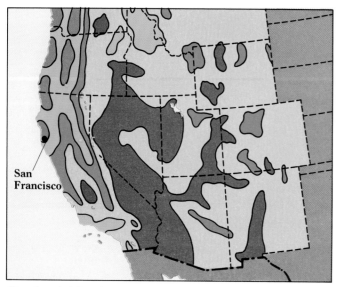

less than 10 inches	
10-20 inches	
20-40 inches	
40-80 inches	
more than 80 inches	

Drylands, steppe	
Desert	
Mediterranean	
Mild, wet	
Mountainous	
Tundra	

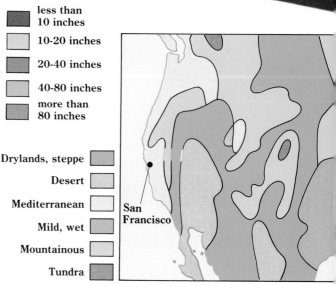

Yearly rainfall varies drastically in the mountainous West.

Mountain ranges divide the western United States into distinct climate zones.

Winds that blow wet and dry

Wet Pacific winds blow inland, where they collide with coastal mountains. Rising, the winds cool, and their moisture turns to rain. The dry winds then continue eastward, wicking up moisture from the Great Basin. At the Rockies, they dump their water again.

California's Death Valley, in the rain shadow of the Panamint Range, is one of the driest places on Earth.

Rocky Mountains

Great Plains

It doesn't get any wetter than this

Mile-high Mt. Waialeale stands like a mammoth sea wall in the path of warm, wet trade winds that buffet Hawaii's Kauai Island. Each year, the winds unload some 500 inches of rain on the mountain's eastern slopes. Then, nearly drained of moisture, the winds move west to shower the town of Kekaha—just 20 miles distant—with a mere 12 inches of annual rainfall.

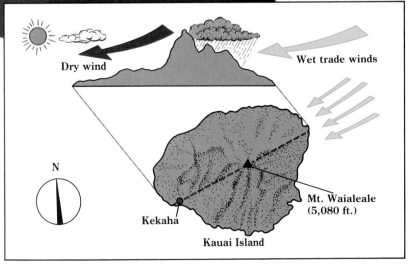

Dry wind

Wet trade winds

N

Kekaha

Mt. Waialeale (5,080 ft.)

Kauai Island

Can Sea Currents Change a Climate?

Though Britain lies as far north as icy Labrador, it enjoys a mild climate. Winter temperatures rarely dip below 35° F., while summer highs seldom top 73° F. The temperate weather is delivered by the North Atlantic Drift, a warm ocean current originating in the tropics.

As the Drift—some 18° F. warmer than the surrounding sea—sweeps past Britain, westerly winds draw heat from the current and blow inland, warming the isles. In summer, the Drift, which is chillier than the land, spawns cooling breezes. In much the same way, ocean currents temper continental climates the world over. The frigid Peru and Benguela currents, for example, cool the western shores of South America and Africa; the California Current brings refreshing winds to the west coast of the United States.

Average temperatures worldwide

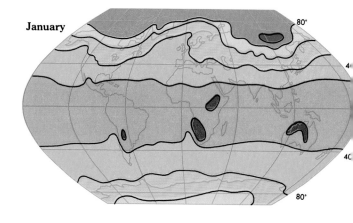

January

Ocean currents and climate

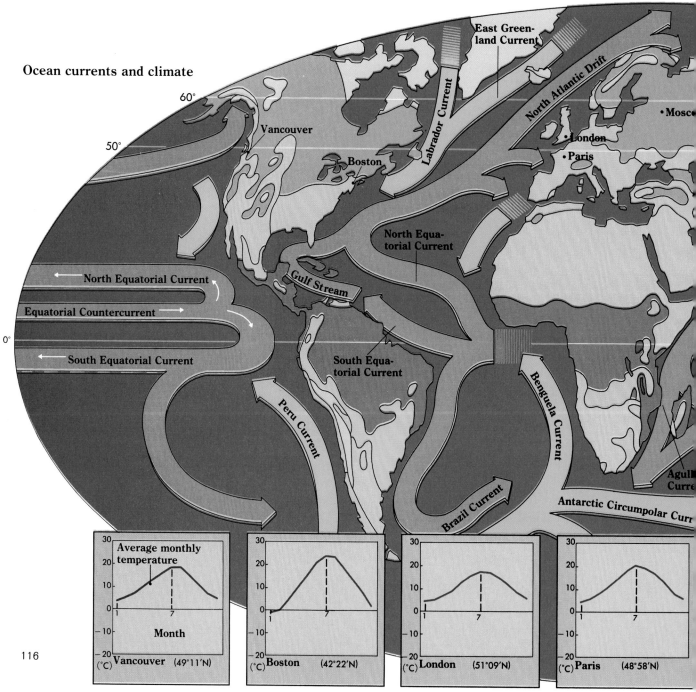

116

A comparison of January temperatures in London, Moscow, and Irkutsk—all at roughly the same latitude—reveals the moderating effect of the North Atlantic Drift. London, at 3.6° C., is 13° warmer than Moscow at −9.4° C., and 23.2° warmer than Irkutsk at −19.6° C.

Same time, different climes: January in London *(above)* . . .

. . . **in Moscow** . . .

. . . **and on Lake Baikal,** near the town of Irkutsk.

July

80°
40°
0°
40°
80°

30
20
0
−20
−30
−40
(°C)

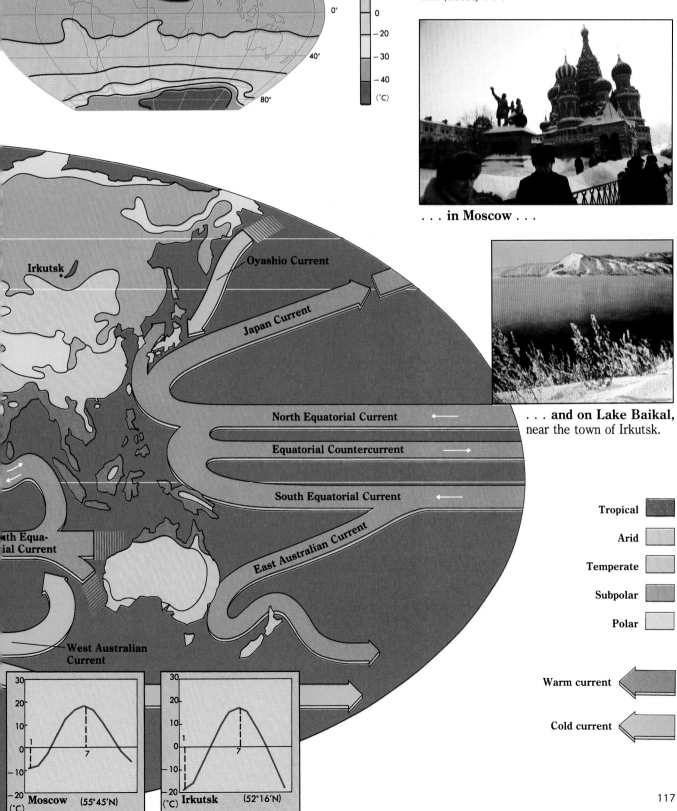

Irkutsk

Oyashio Current

Japan Current

North Equatorial Current

Equatorial Countercurrent

South Equatorial Current

East Australian Current

th Equa-
ial Current

West Australian
Current

Tropical
Arid
Temperate
Subpolar
Polar

Warm current

Cold current

30
20
10
0
−10
−20
(°C)
1
7
Moscow (55°45′N)

30
20
10
0
−10
−20
(°C)
1
7
Irkutsk (52°16′N)

7

The Pace and Price of Progress

Of all the species on Earth, humans have most radically changed their environment to suit their needs. Since people first appeared on the planet, they have striven to make their lives easier and more comfortable. Now, millions of years later, nearly every part of the Earth's face attests to the progress they have made in this respect.

The advances have taken many forms. In the United States, the extensive damming of the Tennessee River in the 1930s and 1940s eventually brought electricity and flood control to an 80,000-square-mile region that covers all of Tennessee and parts of six other southeastern states. In the Netherlands, an elaborate system of dikes built over many centuries has enabled the Dutch people to reclaim more than 1.9 million acres of land from the sea. And thanks to irrigation, once-barren lands now blossom with crops.

Not all progress need be technological, of course; many improvements in the quality of life have resulted from simple human ingenuity. Through careful land use, for example, farmers have boosted the yield of their fields. And by plotting the growth of cities, urban planners hope to anticipate—and avert—the problems created by rapid urban expansion.

Yet progress has a price—chiefly, the degradation of the environment. As the following pages make clear, only prudent planning will enable the human race to enjoy the benefits of progress while minimizing its negative side effects.

Clustered in rings around a nucleus of shops and schools, houses form a regimented pattern in the planned community of Sun City, Arizona.

What Is the Population Explosion?

About 10,000 years ago, scientists estimate, only 8 million humans resided on planet Earth. By AD 1, the population had crept up to about 300 million; it then took until the mid-17th century to double to 600 million. Starting in the 19th century, however, Earth's population exploded. By 1850 the world had 1 billion inhabitants, and by 1930 there were 2 billion. At this exponential rate of growth, the planet could be home to more than 6 billion people by the year 2000 *(time line, below and opposite page)*.

Increased life expectancy is the main reason for the population explosion. As recently as the mid-17th century, the average human being could expect to live for only 40 years. But breakthroughs in medical science and improvements in living conditions over the last few centuries have combined to raise the average worldwide life expectancy to 63.

Economics has also influenced population growth. The population of a country with a strong, stable economy tends to increase slowly, while that of a developing nation tends to grow quickly. This phenomenon has made it especially difficult for developing countries to achieve prosperity and sustained economic growth.

Age, sex, and population

The pyramids on the map below detail the age and sex of various populations. A country like India, whose pyramid is much wider at the bottom than at the top, can expect a large population increase as citizens age. A pyramid with a more uniform shape, such as England's, indicates that stable population growth lies ahead.

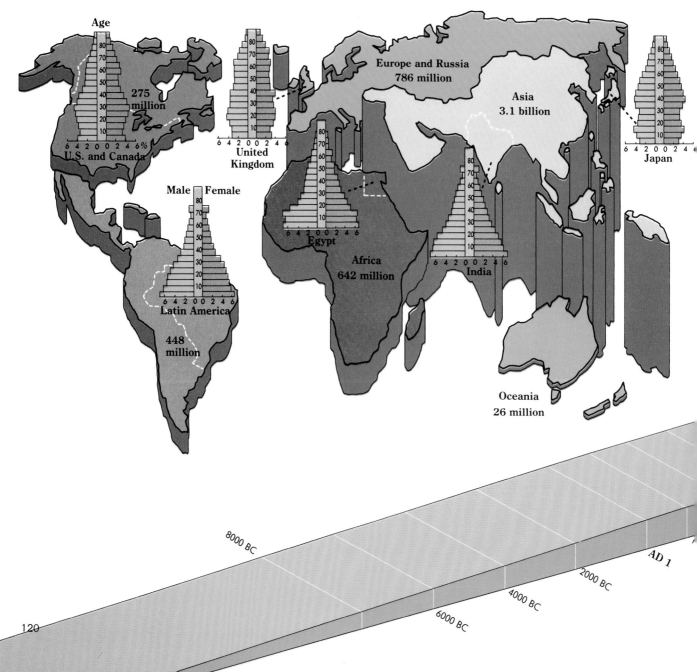

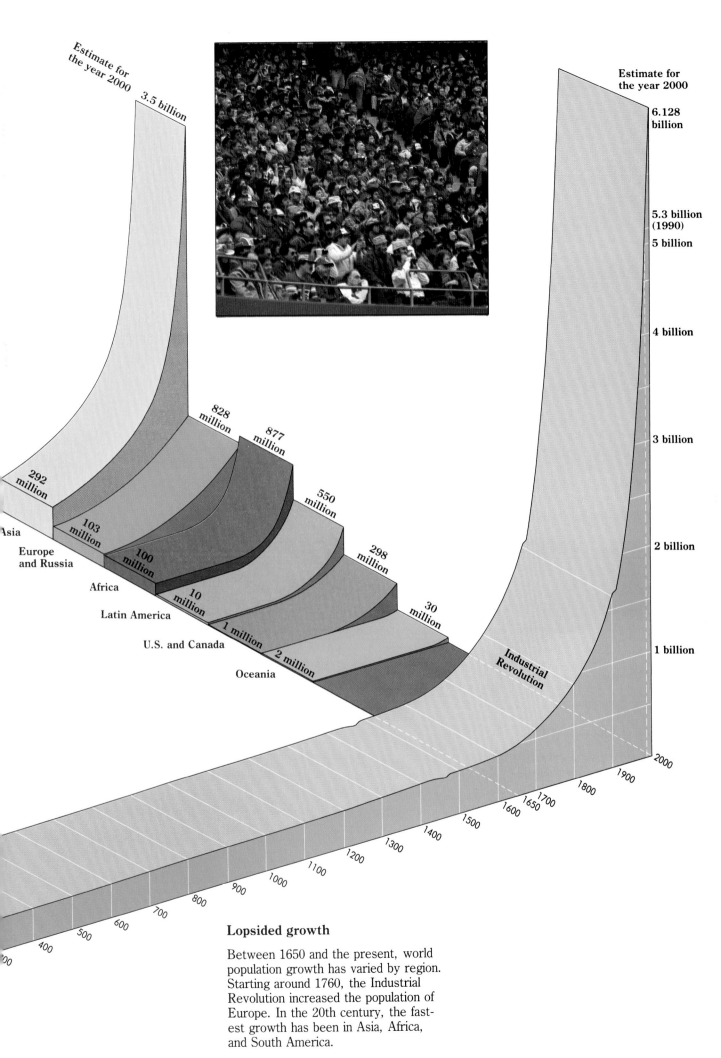

Estimate for
the year 2000
3.5 billion

Estimate for
the year 2000

6.128 billion

5.3 billion (1990)
5 billion

4 billion

3 billion

2 billion

1 billion

828 million

877 million

550 million

292 million

103 million

100 million

298 million

10 million

30 million

1 million

2 million

Asia

Europe and Russia

Africa

Latin America

U.S. and Canada

Oceania

Industrial Revolution

2000

1900

1800

1700
1650

1600

1500

1400

1300

1200

1100

1000

900

800

700

600

500

400

Lopsided growth

Between 1650 and the present, world population growth has varied by region. Starting around 1760, the Industrial Revolution increased the population of Europe. In the 20th century, the fastest growth has been in Asia, Africa, and South America.

121

Where Is Grain Produced?

Three grains—wheat, rice, and corn—supply about half of humanity's nutritional needs. In many countries, a poor harvest of one of these crops may cause severe hardship.

Wheat, an exceptionally hardy plant, is grown in more places than any other grain. It is cultivated on every continent except Antarctica. In most countries, wheat can be grown in spring, summer, and winter. Together the world's wheat fields produce approximately 600 million metric tons of the grain every year.

Rice is the staple food for about half the world's people. More than 95 percent is grown in the Far East, especially India and China, where humidity and fertile coastal lowlands make for ideal growing conditions. Noted for its high yield, rice needs only half as many acres as wheat to produce an equal amount of grain.

Corn production is centered in the United States. Unlike wheat and rice, however, most corn is not consumed by humans; some 80 percent is used to feed livestock or to make products such as corn oil. Roughly 500 million metric tons of corn are grown on the Earth every year.

Rice around the world

■ **Heavy production** □ **Light production**

Villagers harvest rice by hand in a field in Thailand.

Grains of the globe

These bar graphs show the amount of grain that is grown and eaten in various regions the world over. Industrialized nations produce and consume the most grain; they also grow more grain on less land.

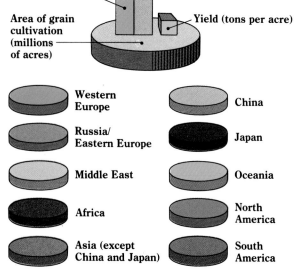

Grain production (millions of tons)

Consumption (millions of tons)

Area of grain cultivation (millions of acres)

Yield (tons per acre)

Western Europe

China

Russia/ Eastern Europe

Japan

Middle East

Oceania

Africa

North America

Asia (except China and Japan)

South America

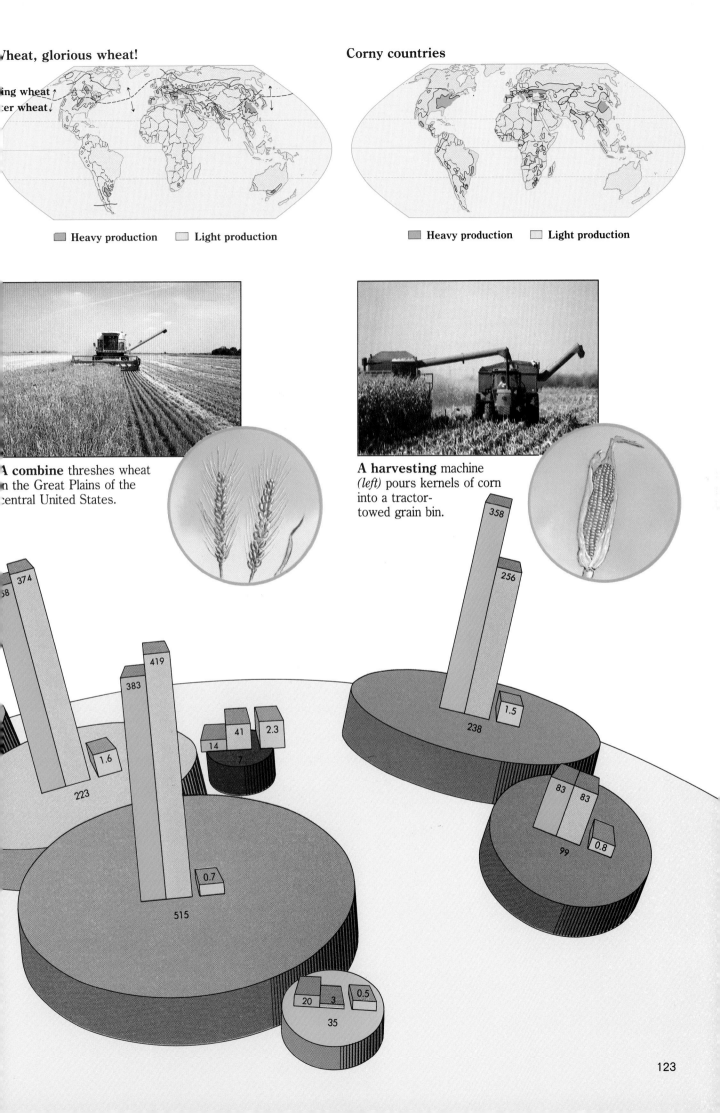

Wheat, glorious wheat!

Spring wheat ↑
Winter wheat ↓

■ Heavy production   ☐ Light production

Corny countries

■ Heavy production   ☐ Light production

A combine threshes wheat on the Great Plains of the central United States.

A harvesting machine (left) pours kernels of corn into a tractor-towed grain bin.

374
58
419
383
223
1.6
14   41   2.3
7
0.7
515
20   3   0.5
35

358
256
1.5
238
83   83
0.8
99

Which Countries Export Lumber?

Although countries rich in trees have always sold lumber to countries that lack them, the areas of supply and demand have changed throughout the 20th century. In 1965, for example, the largest importer of lumber was Great Britain, while the largest exporters were Canada, Finland, Sweden, Russia, and the United States. Today, the biggest importer is Japan. The top exporters are Malaysia, Canada, and Russia, which together account for half the world's total timber exports.

Malaysia's tropical rain forests—a treasure trove of teak, mahogany, and other magnificent hardwoods—resisted large-scale cutting until the 1970s. Before then, loggers were stymied by the sheer variety of trees, which made it hard to sort the timber, and by the difficulty of extricating a hewn tree from the dense, tangled grove in which it grew. With the advent of advanced cutting and processing techniques, however, these obstacles were overcome. By 1990 tropical for-

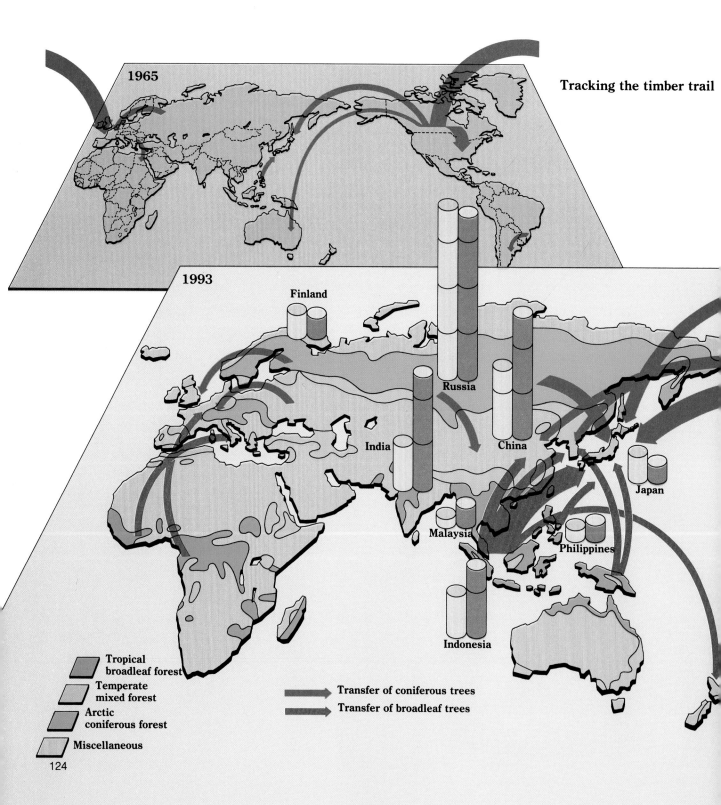

Tracking the timber trail

1965

1993

Finland

Russia

India

China

Japan

Malaysia

Philippines

Indonesia

Tropical broadleaf forest

Temperate mixed forest

Arctic coniferous forest

Miscellaneous

Transfer of coniferous trees

Transfer of broadleaf trees

ests worldwide were being felled at the rate of 42 million acres per year; the loss of oxygen-producing trees at this pace, scientists warn, severely harms the environment.

Lumbermen load logs onto a truck in one of Borneo's tropical rain forests. This form of logging, known as clear-cutting, is extremely destructive.

Canada, covered with coniferous forests like those shown above, is responsible for more than one-fifth of wood exports worldwide.

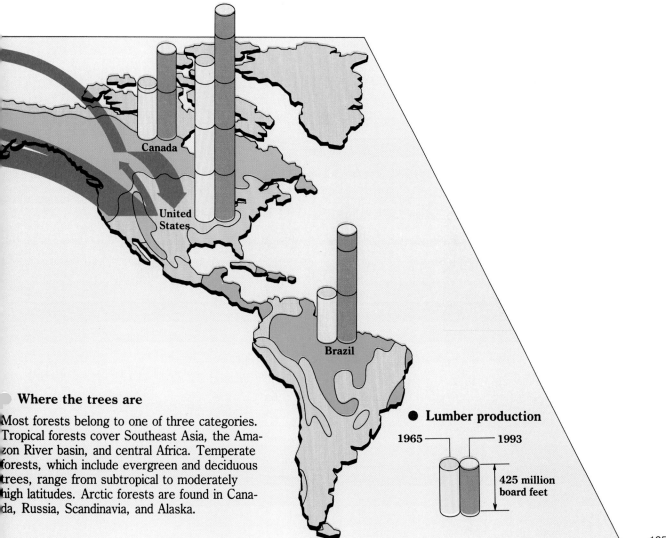

Where the trees are

Most forests belong to one of three categories. Tropical forests cover Southeast Asia, the Amazon River basin, and central Africa. Temperate forests, which include evergreen and deciduous trees, range from subtropical to moderately high latitudes. Arctic forests are found in Canada, Russia, Scandinavia, and Alaska.

● **Lumber production**

1965 ——   —— 1993

425 million board feet

Where Are Most Fish Caught?

Fish roam throughout the world's oceans, but only in a few areas do they gather in numbers high enough to make commercial fishing profitable. For a section of the sea to attract these teeming schools of fish, certain conditions must prevail. If the water is too warm, it will drive off the plankton on which many fish feed. Yet very cold water is inhospitable, too. The most agreeable waters are those in which warm currents and cold currents meet.

Sea depth also dictates where fish congregate. Fish tend to spawn above continental shelves, where the ocean is fairly shallow; such sites therefore make prime fishing grounds.

These two elements—merging currents and broad continental shelves—occur in four major areas: the northwestern, southeastern, and midwestern Pacific Ocean, and the northeastern Atlantic. For nations near these areas, fishing tends to be a major industry—and fish a major food.

The bountiful Atlantic

The waters of northern Europe, where an offshoot of the warm Gulf Stream flows over a broad continental shelf, teem with classic food fish such as cod, herring, and mackerel.

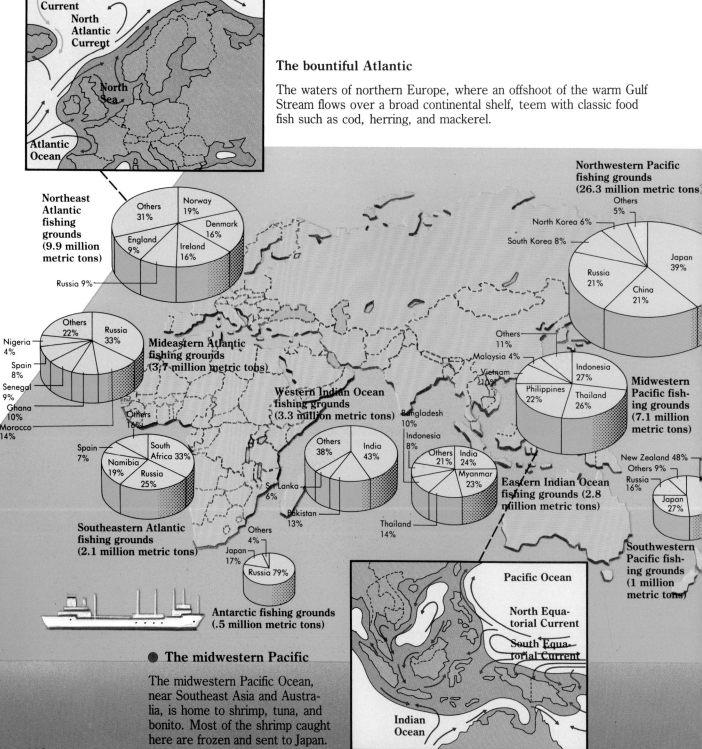

● **The midwestern Pacific**

The midwestern Pacific Ocean, near Southeast Asia and Australia, is home to shrimp, tuna, and bonito. Most of the shrimp caught here are frozen and sent to Japan.

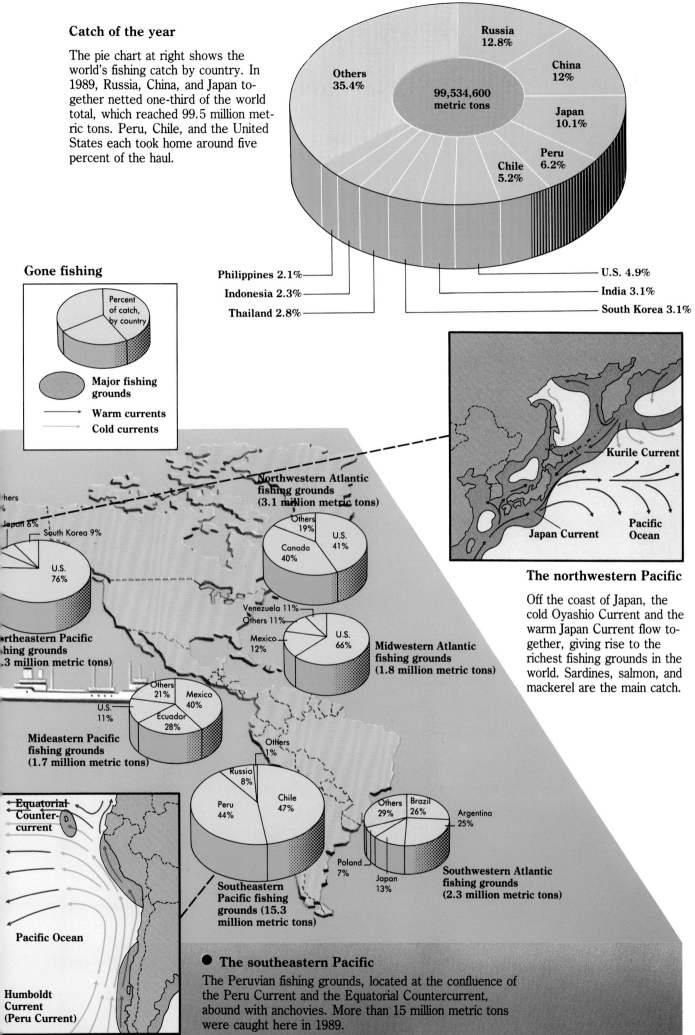

Catch of the year

The pie chart at right shows the world's fishing catch by country. In 1989, Russia, China, and Japan together netted one-third of the world total, which reached 99.5 million metric tons. Peru, Chile, and the United States each took home around five percent of the haul.

Russia 12.8%
China 12%
Japan 10.1%
Peru 6.2%
Chile 5.2%
Others 35.4%

99,534,600 metric tons

Philippines 2.1%
Indonesia 2.3%
Thailand 2.8%

U.S. 4.9%
India 3.1%
South Korea 3.1%

Gone fishing

Percent of catch, by country

Major fishing grounds

→ Warm currents

→ Cold currents

Kurile Current

Japan Current

Pacific Ocean

The northwestern Pacific

Off the coast of Japan, the cold Oyashio Current and the warm Japan Current flow together, giving rise to the richest fishing grounds in the world. Sardines, salmon, and mackerel are the main catch.

Northwestern Atlantic fishing grounds (3.1 million metric tons)
Others 19%
U.S. 41%
Canada 40%

...hers %
Japan 6%
South Korea 9%
U.S. 76%

...rtheastern Pacific ...hing grounds .3 million metric tons)

Venezuela 11%
Others 11%
Mexico 12%
U.S. 66%
Midwestern Atlantic fishing grounds (1.8 million metric tons)

Others 21%
Mexico 40%
U.S. 11%
Ecuador 28%

Mideastern Pacific fishing grounds (1.7 million metric tons)

Others 1%
Russia 8%
Peru 44%
Chile 47%

Others 29%
Brazil 26%
Argentina 25%
Poland 7%
Japan 13%
Southwestern Atlantic fishing grounds (2.3 million metric tons)

Southeastern Pacific fishing grounds (15.3 million metric tons)

← Equatorial Counter-current

Pacific Ocean

Humboldt Current (Peru Current)

● The southeastern Pacific

The Peruvian fishing grounds, located at the confluence of the Peru Current and the Equatorial Countercurrent, abound with anchovies. More than 15 million metric tons were caught here in 1989.

What Is a Planned City?

Most of the world's cities developed slowly over decades or centuries, with no master plan to guide their growth. A few, however, have taken shape according to careful schemes. In these communities, known as planned cities, every aspect of urban life is anticipated in an overall design before the first building goes up.

In contrast to the gridiron layout of many unplanned cities, a planned city typically features a radial street plan, in which broad avenues lead outward from spacious parks. The Australian capital of Canberra, designed in 1911, is a good example of the success of this approach.

The lessons learned in planning a future city can benefit a city that already exists. London, for instance, adopted a plan for controlled expansion during the 1930s and 1940s that preserved a 10-mile-wide "green belt" of parkland around the metropolis. Although the English capital had 9.1 million inhabitants by 1991, its population density was just 10,429 residents per square mile—almost 25 times sparser than Hong Kong.

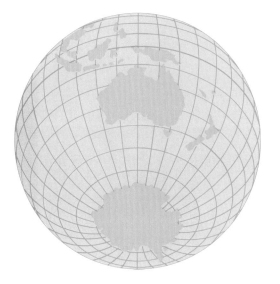

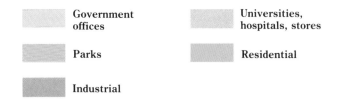

Government offices

Universities, hospitals, stores

Parks

Residential

Industrial

A city that can bear a second look

Lake Burley Griffin—named for Canberra's designer, Chicago landscape architect Walter Burley Griffin—splits the Australian capital city *(opposite)* into two zones. Most of the government buildings cluster in the triangle formed by Commonwealth Avenue and Kings Avenue. Residential, educational, cultural, and commercial districts are scattered throughout the city. The bulk of Canberra's industries are confined to an area around the train station just south of the East Basin.

The benefits of planning ahead

Standing atop 2,762-foot Mount Ainslie, two visitors survey the planned city of Canberra in southeastern Australia. Directly below them is the green dome of the Australian-American War Memorial; beyond that, a wide avenue called the Anzac Parade leads to man-made Lake Burley Griffin. In line with the Anzac Parade on the lake's far shore is the old Parliament House; directly behind it, on top of Capital Hill, stands the new Parliament House. Although Canberra has a population of nearly 300,000, one observer noted that "there's still enough space between buildings to make the city seem more like a gigantic college campus than a teeming metropolis."

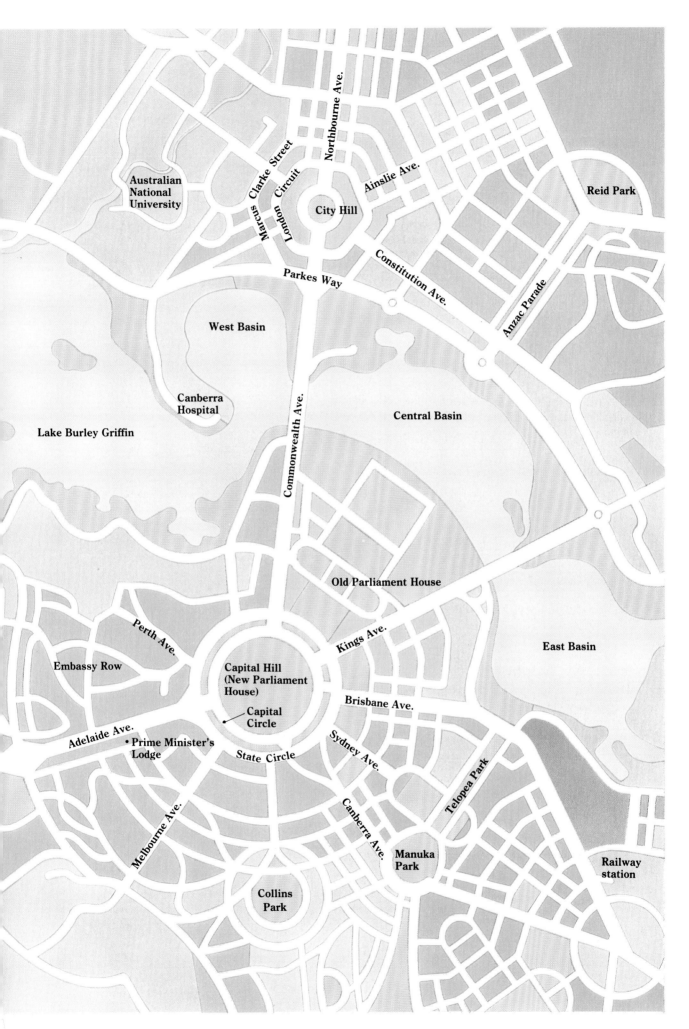

Are All Farms the Same?

The agriculture of a region depends mainly on its climate. Crops that need a great deal of water—rice and fruits such as mangoes and bananas—grow well in the rain-swept tropics. Crops such as wheat, barley, rye, and oats, which need less water, flourish in drier, temperate areas. And root crops such as sweet potatoes and cassavas can survive lingering drought once their growth is established. Other factors governing the success of a crop include the region's temperature, soil quality, length of daylight, and type of terrain.

Millions of acres under tillage today were once deemed impossible to farm. They may have been too dry, too hilly, or too poor in nutrients to permit easy cultivation. Using techniques such as irrigation, terracing, and fertilization, however, local farmers have transformed these barren tracts into bountiful fields.

In 1936 a Harvard geography professor named Derwent Whittlesey devised a system for classifying land according to its agricultural potential. Whittlesey's 13 zones, shown on the map at right, give a good idea of land-use patterns worldwide.

World agricultural zones

The map at right classifies the planet's agricultural lands according to the Whittlesey system. Innovative techniques have made increasing amounts of Earth's land surface suitable for some form of farming.

Grazing	Extensive settlement agriculture
Commercial cattle raising	Self-sufficient paddy agriculture
Nomadic cultivation	Self-sufficient agriculture without paddies

Cattle await shipping from a Midwest stockyard. More than 1.3 billion head of cattle are raised worldwide. The major cattle-ranching countries are Brazil, the United States, Russia, China, India, and Argentina.

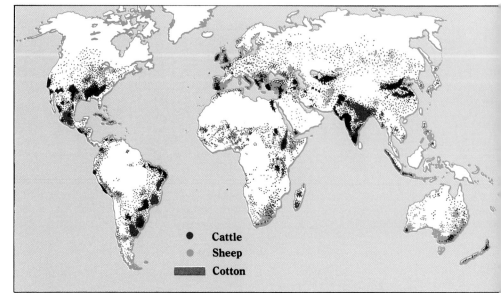

- Cattle
- Sheep
- Cotton

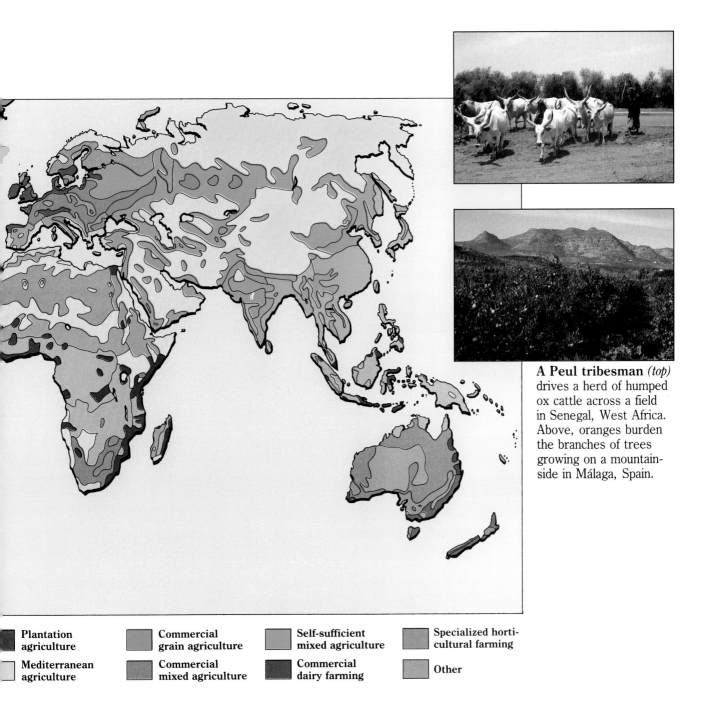

A Peul tribesman *(top)* drives a herd of humped ox cattle across a field in Senegal, West Africa. Above, oranges burden the branches of trees growing on a mountainside in Málaga, Spain.

■ Plantation agriculture

■ Commercial grain agriculture

■ Self-sufficient mixed agriculture

■ Specialized horticultural farming

□ Mediterranean agriculture

■ Commercial mixed agriculture

■ Commercial dairy farming

■ Other

mechanized cotton picker moves [th]rough a Missouri field. In decreas[in]g order of output, China, the United [St]ates, Russia, India, and Pakistan [ar]e the world's major cotton growers.

A sheepdog corrals a herd in Australia, home to 20 percent of the world's population of 150 million sheep. Russia, China, New Zealand, India, and Turkey also support large numbers of the animals, which are raised for both wool and meat.

Orderly rows of olive trees soak up sunshine on the island of Sicily in the Mediterranean Sea.

Can Land Be "Saved" from the Sea?

Lack of space is a fact of life in the Netherlands, where 15 million people live in an area half the size of West Virginia. Through centuries of ingenious engineering, however, Holland has reclaimed nearly two million acres of land that were once covered by the sea.

Starting in about 450 BC, the area's earliest settlers started building small hills, called *terpen,* that kept their farms above the high tides and floods that periodically swamped the land. In the 12th century, farmers began to connect the terpen with water-blocking bulwarks, called dikes. The area girded by a dike could then be drained by canals or by windmill-driven pumps. As the seawater receded, it exposed land suitable for farming. Dike building in Holland reached its zenith in 1932, when the government completed a 19-mile-long dam across the mouth of the Zuider Zee that has increased the country's land area by 626 square miles, or almost five percent.

Holland's battle with the sea

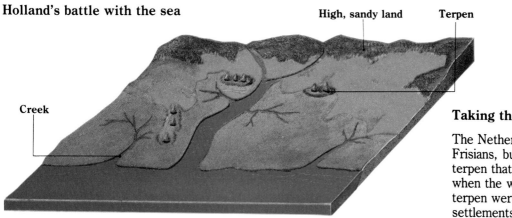

High, sandy land   Terpen

Creek

Taking the first steps

The Netherlands' early inhabitants, the Frisians, built earthen hillocks called terpen that kept them high and dry when the waters rose. In time, the terpen were enlarged to support entire settlements.

Drainage floodgate

Building dikes

Earthworks were built to link terpen, creating dikes. Farmers then drained the land surrounded by the dikes. At low tide, drainage holes (and, later, floodgates) were opened to release any water that had breached the dikes during high tide.

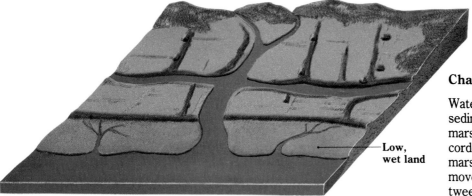

Low, wet land

Channeling the water inland

Water outside the dikes deposited sediments that accumulated to form marshes. New dikes were built to cordon off the marshes, and the marshes were drained. Seawater moved inland through channels between the dikes.

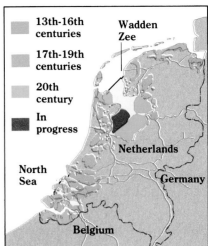

Stemming the tides

To prevent flooding during heavy storms or unusually high tides, dams were constructed across the mouths of the inland waterways.

About 19 percent of present-day Holland consists of land that has been reclaimed from the sea.

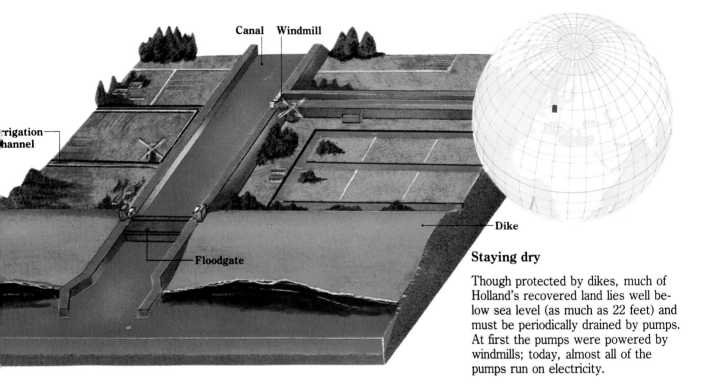

Staying dry

Though protected by dikes, much of Holland's recovered land lies well below sea level (as much as 22 feet) and must be periodically drained by pumps. At first the pumps were powered by windmills; today, almost all of the pumps run on electricity.

The low profile of the Low Countries

A cross-sectional view of the northern Netherlands *(below)* shows the country's various types of recovered land, called polder. Most early polders have poor drainage and are now used for dairy farming; newer polders are used mainly for growing crops. Lake Ijssel is a 300,000-acre body of water that was created by damming the former Zuider Zee. North of the Afsluitdijk, or great barrier dam, lies a body of seawater known as the Wadden Zee.

Roads travel the tops of many dikes; the one above crosses the dam that created Lake Ijssel.

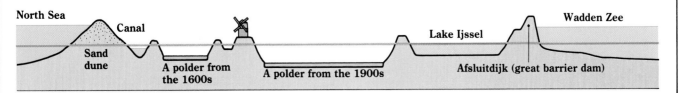

What Is the Tennessee Valley Authority?

In 1933 the U.S. Congress created the Tennessee Valley Authority (TVA) and charged it with developing the natural resources of the Tennessee River valley. Since then, the TVA has constructed or acquired 39 dams, two nuclear power plants, and 11 coal-fired plants along the Tennessee River and its tributaries. As a result, TVA projects deliver more than 100 billion kilowatt-hours of electricity each year to an area that covers 80,000 square miles and spans seven states—Tennessee, Kentucky, Virginia, North Carolina, Georgia, Alabama, and Mississippi.

From Paducah, Kentucky, to Knoxville, Tennessee, TVA dams have turned the Tennessee River into a 650-mile chain of lakes. Kentucky Lake, the largest, is 185 miles long. The lakes are connected by a system of locks, so the entire waterway is navigable by barges with a draft of up to 9 feet.

The success of the TVA in providing inexpensive electric power to a large area has been duplicated elsewhere, notably in the Colorado and Columbia river valleys. Overseas, major river-development projects are in place on the Mekong River in Southeast Asia, the Damodar in India, and the Nile in Egypt.

Norris Dam, rising 265 feet above the Clinch River in Tennessee, was the TVA's first hydroelectric dam.

Fontana Dam's power station, shown above, sits beside North Carolina's Little Tennessee River.

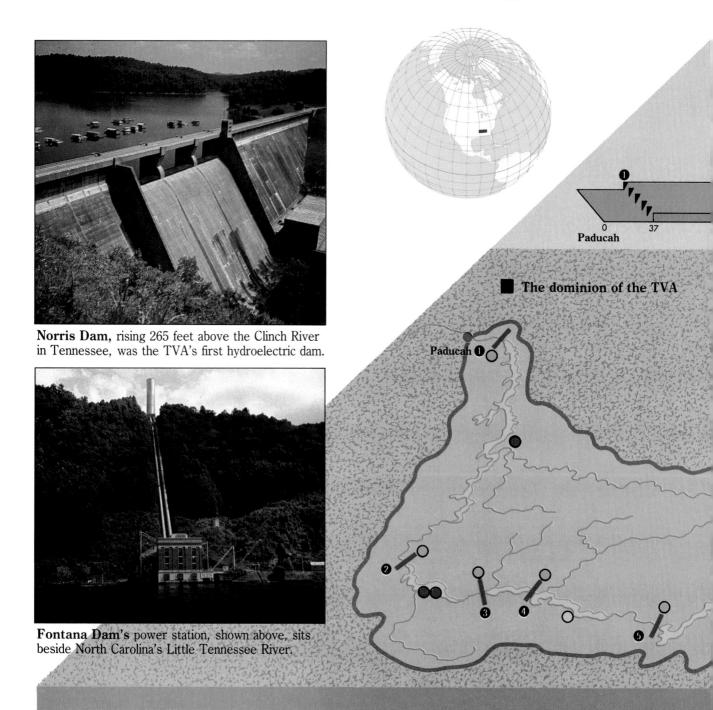

Paducah

■ **The dominion of the TVA**

Paducah

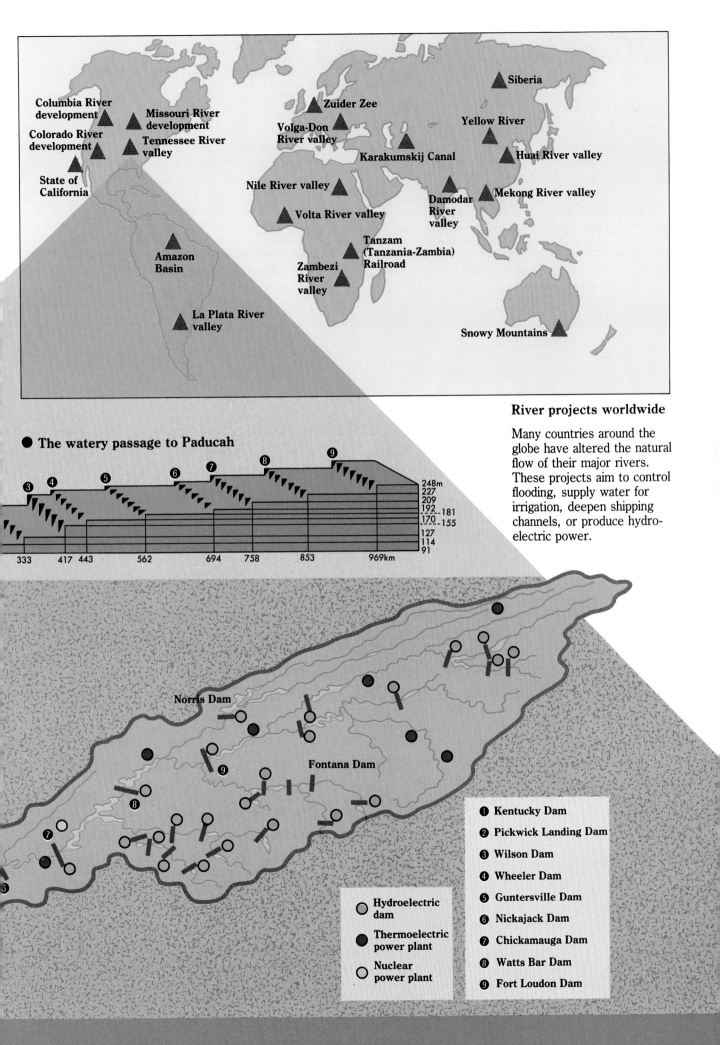

Columbia River development

Colorado River development

State of California

Missouri River development

Tennessee River valley

Amazon Basin

La Plata River valley

Zuider Zee

Volga-Don River valley

Karakumskij Canal

Nile River valley

Volta River valley

Zambezi River valley

Tanzam (Tanzania-Zambia) Railroad

Siberia

Yellow River

Huai River valley

Damodar River valley

Mekong River valley

Snowy Mountains

● **The watery passage to Paducah**

③ ④ ⑤ ⑥ ⑦ ⑧ ⑨

248m
227
209
192 181
170 155
127
114
91

333 417 443 562 694 758 853 969km

River projects worldwide

Many countries around the globe have altered the natural flow of their major rivers. These projects aim to control flooding, supply water for irrigation, deepen shipping channels, or produce hydro-electric power.

Norris Dam

⑨

Fontana Dam

⑧

⑦

Hydroelectric dam

Thermoelectric power plant

Nuclear power plant

❶ Kentucky Dam

❷ Pickwick Landing Dam

❸ Wilson Dam

❹ Wheeler Dam

❺ Guntersville Dam

❻ Nickajack Dam

❼ Chickamauga Dam

❽ Watts Bar Dam

❾ Fort Loudon Dam

Where Do Grapes and Olives Grow?

Olives and grapes grow in abundance in every country that borders the Mediterranean Sea. The trees and vines have been cultivated in this area since at least 3000 BC because they are ideally suited to the Mediterranean climate.

Although the Mediterranean basin enjoys mild, moist winters, it is also famous for its hot, dry summers. For a plant to flourish in this environment, it must be able to withstand spells of drought until the rainy season returns. This is no problem for olive trees, which actually prefer dry conditions. Grapevines, too, can easily survive the lack of precipitation; to reach the layers of moist soil that lie deep beneath the surface, their taproots can grow up to 100 feet long.

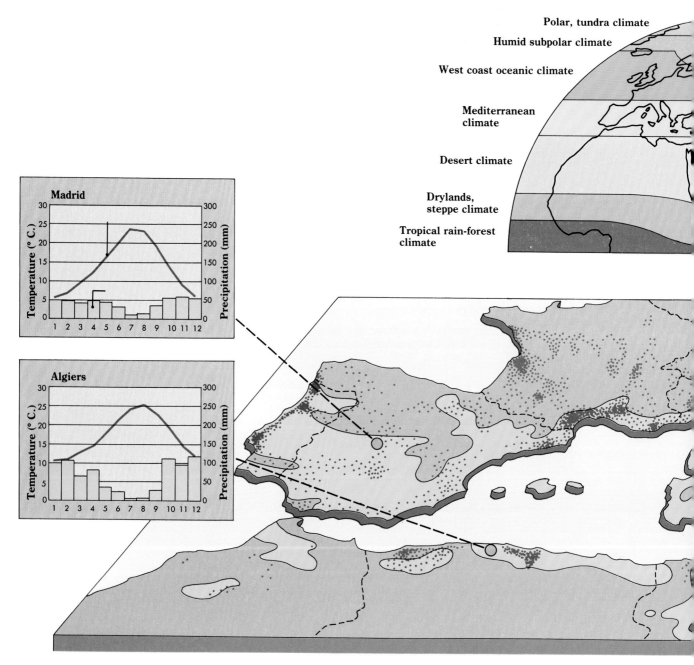

A fruit-filled basin

Six Mediterranean countries—Spain, Italy, Greece, Portugal, Tunisia, and Turkey—together account for 94 percent of the world's olive output. As shown above, most of the olive groves cluster near the coast; grapes, however, can be grown as far north as Germany. Europe produces 75 percent of the world's grape harvest.

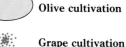

Olive cultivation

Grape cultivation

Crops and weather

In summer, the Mediterranean coast is blanketed by a zone of high pressure that keeps the area warm and dry. In winter, by contrast, low-pressure winds blowing from the west bring steady rains. Grapevines and olive trees both thrive under these conditions.

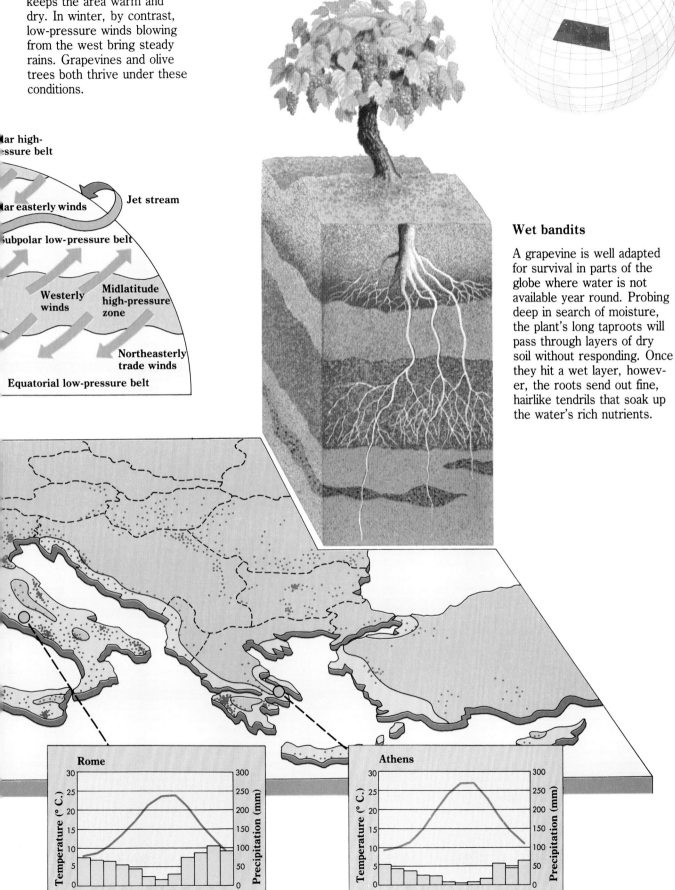

Polar high-pressure belt

Polar easterly winds

Jet stream

Subpolar low-pressure belt

Westerly winds

Midlatitude high-pressure zone

Northeasterly trade winds

Equatorial low-pressure belt

Wet bandits

A grapevine is well adapted for survival in parts of the globe where water is not available year round. Probing deep in search of moisture, the plant's long taproots will pass through layers of dry soil without responding. Once they hit a wet layer, however, the roots send out fine, hairlike tendrils that soak up the water's rich nutrients.

Rome

Temperature (° C.)

Precipitation (mm)

1 2 3 4 5 6 7 8 9 10 11 12

Athens

Temperature (° C.)

Precipitation (mm)

1 2 3 4 5 6 7 8 9 10 11 12

Can Arid Lands Be Farmed?

Farmers have devised two tactics for growing crops on land that gets little rain. In the first, called dryland farming, crops are planted on only half of a farm; the other half is deeply plowed, then left fallow so that any rainfall will sink into—and be retained by—the soil. After soaking up precious moisture for a year, the fallow land is planted with crops, while the cultivated acres are harvested and allowed to rest.

The second technique is irrigation, or channeling water from places where it is plentiful to fields where it is not. Irrigation has transformed once-barren areas such as California's Imperial Valley and Israel's Negev desert region into rich farmland. As shown on these pages, irrigation takes many forms. The water may be piped in from distant lakes, for example, or a river may be dammed to create a water source close by.

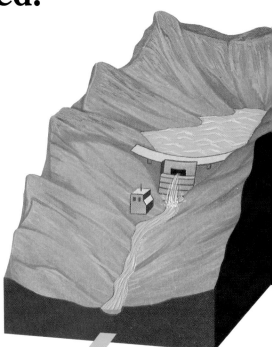

Making the desert bloom

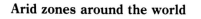

Arid zones around the world

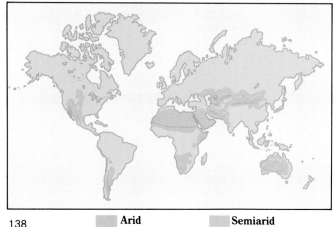

138   ▮ **Arid**   ▮ **Semiarid**

Circular fields, each watered by a center-pivot irrigation pipe, pockmark a corner of Utah.

An artificial lake

Damming a mountain stream or river creates a year-round supply of water for irrigation. However, the dam may disrupt the environment of regions that lie downstream.

A life-giving pipeline

When impassable terrain lies between arid farmland and the nearest source of irrigation water, the water may be transported to its destination by a pumping station and pipeline *(left)*.

Tapping an underground source

In arid regions of China, Pakistan, Iran, and North Africa, farmers irrigate their fields using *kanats*—channels that draw water from beneath the ground near the base of a mountain. Vertical shafts drilled into the hillside provide ventilation and access for repairs.

Well water

Even the driest land may conceal a source of water, which can be pumped from a well *(left)*. Artesian wells flow without pumping.

Access holes demarcate a kanat in Pakistan.

What Is the Altiplano?

The Andes mountain range forms the spine of South America. Running more than 4,500 miles from Colombia to Cape Horn, it shapes the geography and climate of the entire continent. A dramatic example of its influence can be found in Argentina and landlocked Bolivia, where the Andes reach their widest extent (400 miles) and a broad, high plain called the Altiplano lies suspended between parallel mountain ridges. Thanks to the moderating influence of nearby Lake Titicaca—at 3,500 square miles, the largest lake in South America—the Altiplano enjoys some unusually mild weather for an area of such extreme elevation (13,000 feet, on average).

The southern part of the Bolivian Altiplano gets so little precipitation that salt flats dot the barren, rocky land. The northern part, however, has a more moderate climate, making it the area's center of farming. (Indeed, the Altiplano may be the original home of the potato.) Soaring to nearly 16,000 feet above sea level are the high plains of a third region, the puna. Because of its great altitude, the puna is too cold for farming; however, it is covered with a coarse, bristly grass called *ichu,* which supports large herds of llamas and their cousins, the alpacas and vicunas. The wool of these animals can be traded for products from the Pacific coast—sea salt, chili peppers, and fruit—while the beasts themselves serve to transport the goods.

A land above the clouds

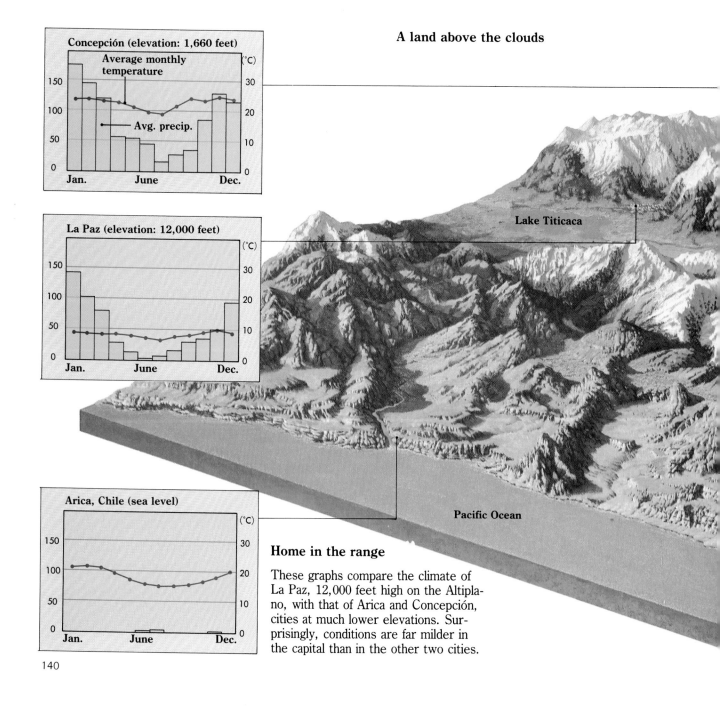

Home in the range

These graphs compare the climate of La Paz, 12,000 feet high on the Altiplano, with that of Arica and Concepción, cities at much lower elevations. Surprisingly, conditions are far milder in the capital than in the other two cities.

A sunray hits the mountains of La Paz.

Farms are terraced near Lake Titicaca.

Bolivian llamas graze on ichu grass.

An Indian pulls reeds from Titicaca.

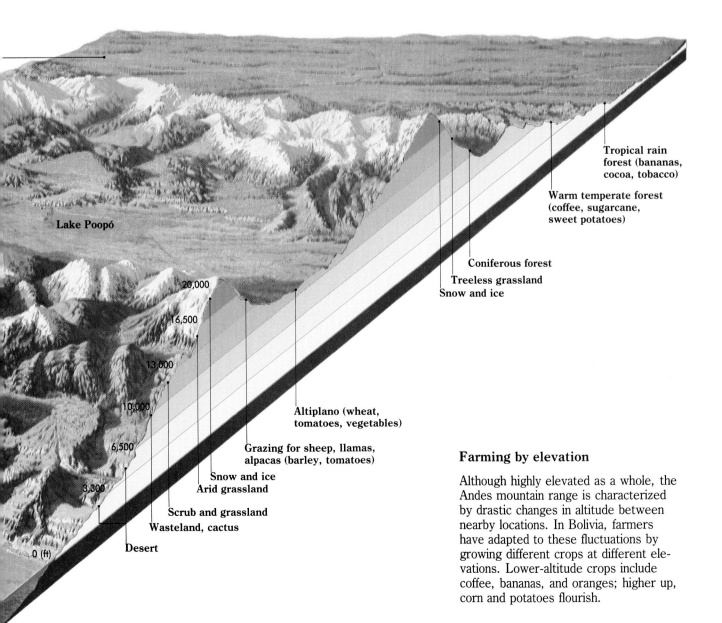

Lake Poopó

Tropical rain forest (bananas, cocoa, tobacco)

Warm temperate forest (coffee, sugarcane, sweet potatoes)

Coniferous forest
Treeless grassland
Snow and ice

20,000

16,500

13,000

10,000

Altiplano (wheat, tomatoes, vegetables)

6,500

Grazing for sheep, llamas, alpacas (barley, tomatoes)

3,300

Snow and ice
Arid grassland

Scrub and grassland

Wasteland, cactus

Desert

0 (ft)

Farming by elevation

Although highly elevated as a whole, the Andes mountain range is characterized by drastic changes in altitude between nearby locations. In Bolivia, farmers have adapted to these fluctuations by growing different crops at different elevations. Lower-altitude crops include coffee, bananas, and oranges; higher up, corn and potatoes flourish.

Can One Place Have Many Climates?

With five peaks rising more than 14,000 feet high, the Alps are Europe's biggest mountain chain. So great is the altitude variance between the valleys and the mountaintops that the region has four separate climates. The coldest climate prevails at the highest elevations; known collectively as the firn zone, these areas are blanketed with a permanent layer of snow that has compacted into glacial ice. Below the firn zone is the alpine zone, whose meadows make good pastureland. The subalpine zone, closer to sea level, is covered with carefully conserved coniferous forests. The arable zone, lowest of the four, is dotted with villages and deciduous trees.

Many residents of these villages raise livestock, using a technique called transhumance to accommodate the region's varying climates. In winter, the sheep and cattle are kept in barns and fed with stored hay. In the spring, the herds are led to pastures in the higher climate zones, where they graze through the summer before being led back down in the fall.

The hills are alive

The vegetation of the Alps varies with altitude. Very few plants exist in the firn zone, above 10,000 feet. Alpine wildflowers and grasses grow in the alpine zone, between 6,500 and 10,000 feet. The subalpine zone, 5,000 to 6,500 feet high, is home to forests of fir and spruce. Below 5,000 feet lie dense stands of oak and beech trees.

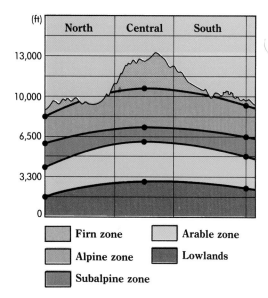

Flowers carpet an alpine meadow near the base of Switzerland's 14,780-foot-high Matterhorn.

Going for the green

10,000 ft

7,200-10,000 ft

5,300-7,200 ft

4,300-5,300 ft

4,300 ft

1. Shepherd's hut
2. Pasture used in July and August
3. Pasture used in June
4. Pasture used in May and September
5. Pasture used in April and October
6. Pasture used from November to March

Cattle graze in an Alpine pasture in Switzerland.

143

Are We Running Out of Land?

Faced with the need to build a large new airport in an area where open land is scarce, Japanese planners came up with a novel solution: The Kansai International Airport is being constructed on an artificial landfill in Osaka Bay, three miles off the shore of Japan's second-largest city.

Building the airport was an unprecedented engineering challenge. First, workers stabilized the seabed foundation by driving piles of hardened sand into the soft clay that lies 59 feet below the water's surface. A sea wall was then erected around the foundation, creating a 1,263-acre area that was filled with soil and rock to raise it above sea level. Work then began on the airport itself, which will be joined to the mainland by a double-decker rail-and-auto bridge.

Building a strong foundation

To lay the airport's underwater foundation, marine engineers drove piles into the soft clay of Osaka Bay.

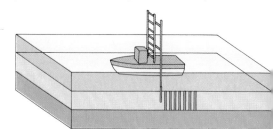

Filling in the gaps

After the foundation and sea wall had been built, barges dumped 220 million cubic yards of rock and soil inside the wall.

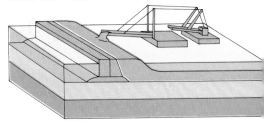

A satellite photo of Osaka Bay *(above)* reveals the offshore site of Kansai International Airport.

Glossary

Abyssal: Describing areas of great depth in oceans or lakes or within the Earth.

Alluvium: Any unconsolidated sediment, such as clay, silt, sand, or gravel, that is deposited by rivers or streams.

Alpine: Relating to high elevations, usually above the timberline, where trees cannot grow.

Aquifer: A rock formation below the surface of the Earth that holds water.

Artesian: A word used to describe ground water under such pressure that it rises above the aquifer containing it. An **artesian spring** is a naturally flowing stream of water that comes out of rock overlying the aquifer. An **artesian well** is a human-made well from which water need not be pumped; instead, it bubbles up like a fountain.

Bedrock: Solid rock that lies beneath a covering of soil or is exposed at the Earth's surface.

Broadleaf: Describing a tree whose leaves are not needles.

Butte: A flat-topped isolated hill or small mountain whose steep sides rise abruptly above the surrounding terrain; a small mesa.

Canyon: A chasm, cut into the Earth's surface by a river, with cliffs rising on either side.

Cartography: The art and science of making maps.

Cirque: A steep-walled, amphitheater-like basin high on the side of a mountain, caused by glacial erosion.

Clay: A sediment made up of very fine particles, with a consistency like that of putty or soft plastic.

Climate: The long-term weather patterns of a region.

Conifer: A cone-bearing seed plant, such as a pine tree, with mostly evergreen needles or scalelike leaves.

Continental drift: The theory that the continents ride on giant plates, which glide and move very slowly across the surface of the Earth.

Continental margin: The zone that separates a continent from the deep ocean floor. It includes the **continental shelf,** a shallow, gradually sloping area that extends about 40 miles from the shore; the **continental slope,** a steep incline that descends from the continental shelf to the deep sea bottom; and the **continental rise,** a gentle incline at the base of the continental slope.

Coriolis effect: An apparent force, produced by the rotation of the Earth, that causes the path of moving objects to veer away from a straight line. The Coriolis effect explains why winds and ocean currents curve to the right (clockwise) in the Northern Hemisphere and to the left (counterclockwise) in the Southern Hemisphere.

Cuesta: A rock outcropping with a gently sloping surface on one side and a steep cliff on the other.

Current: A continuous flow, in a steady direction, of water or other liquids, or of gases such as air.

Delta: A low, nearly flat, triangle-shaped plain of alluvial deposits at the mouth of a river.

Desert: An area in which the annual precipitation is 10 inches or less, making the region generally incapable of supporting large populations of plants or animals.

Drumlin: A low, elongate, streamlined hill made of rocks, soil, and other debris deposited by a glacier as it advanced. Drumlins indicate the path taken by a glacier that has since melted.

Environment: The climate, soil, and living things with which an organism interacts and which determine its form and survival.

Equator: An imaginary line that circles the Earth at its widest part, precisely halfway between the North and South poles. The equator lies at 0° latitude.

Erosion: The process by which soil or rock is worn away and moved elsewhere by water, wind, or ice.

Esker: A long, winding ridge of sand or gravel laid down by a stream flowing under or through a glacier.

Estuary: The seaward end of a river valley, where fresh water from a river mixes with salt water from the sea.

Fallow: Farmland that is left unseeded during a growing season.

Fissure: A long, narrow, deep crack in rock or ice.

Geography: The study of Earth's surface features, including the distribution and interrelations of elements such as plant and animal life, soil, elevation, population, industry, and political divisions.

Geology: The study of Earth's history, internal makeup, and external features, with an emphasis on the rocks and minerals that compose the planet and the processes that have shaped it.

Glacier: A mass of ice, produced by the accumulation and compaction of snow, that moves downhill or outward from its center.

Guyot: A flat-topped mountain submerged in an ocean.

Gyre: A circular movement of ocean currents, turning clockwise in the Northern Hemisphere and counterclockwise in the Southern Hemisphere.

Horn: A high, sharp peak with steep sides, occurring at the intersection of three or more cirques.

Igneous rock: Rock that has crystallized from a molten state. Igneous rock is one of the three major kinds of rock; the others are sedimentary rock and metamorphic rock.

Influent stream: A stream whose channel lies above the water table. Influent streams contribute water to the ground-water system.

International Date Line: A longitudinal line that follows the 180th meridian. It is the point at which each new calendar day begins.

Karren: Furrows that occur in limestone as rainwater dissolves the surface.

Karst: A type of landscape formed on limestone or gypsum and characterized by sinkholes, caves, and underground drainage.

Lagoon: A shallow body of water with a restricted opening to the ocean. A lagoon's entrance is constricted by a reef or by a sand bar.

Latitude: The angular distance of a point on the Earth's surface from the equator, expressed in degrees north or south. Degrees of latitude begin at the equator (0° latitude) and are measured northward to the North Pole (90° north latitude) and southward to the South Pole (90° south latitude).

Loess: A thick deposit of yellowish, very fine particles of clay, silt, and sand that results from wind erosion.

Longitude: The angular distance of a point on the Earth's surface from a north-south reference line called the prime meridian. Longitude is expressed in degrees east or west.

Map: The representation of the Earth's three-dimensional surface features on a flat (two-dimensional) surface.

Meander: Any one of a series of long, looping bends in the course of a river.

Meridian: An imaginary circle on the surface of the Earth that passes through both the North and South poles. Meridians run perpendicular to the equator and all other lines of latitude.

Mesa: A flat-topped isolated mountain surrounded by steep cliffs.

Metamorphic rock: A rock whose composition, structure, or texture has been transformed without melting by heat, pressure, or chemical action. Metamorphic is one of the three major types of rock; the others are igneous and sedimentary.

Moraine: A ridge or mound of debris deposited by glacial activity. A **lateral moraine** consists of debris deposited at the sides of a glacier; a **medial moraine** forms along the line where two glaciers meet and merge; a **recessional moraine** takes shape where a melting glacier pauses in its retreat; a **terminal moraine** marks the glacier's farthest downslope advance; and **ground moraine** is deposited on the land over which the glacier moves.

Mountain: Any part of the Earth's crust that rises significantly—say 1,000 feet or more—above the surrounding land.

Nautical chart: A map used to guide sailors safely through harbors or across oceans and other bodies of water.

Ocean: The large bodies of salt water that together cover two-thirds of the Earth's surface.

Oceanic ridge: The underwater mountain range where new oceanic crust is constantly being generated and pushed outward through the process of seafloor spreading.

Oxbow lake: A crescent-shaped lake formed when a meander, or river bend, becomes cut off over time from the river's main course.

Plain: A vast expanse of generally flat land.

Plate tectonics: The theory that the Earth's crust consists of rigid plates in constant motion. The resultant colliding, grinding, and separating motions produce intense geological activity at the edges of the plates.

Prairie: A series of extensive grasslands in the Mississippi River valley that boast deep, fertile soil and tall grasses, but few trees.

Prime meridian: The imaginary line at 0° longitude that connects the North and South poles via the Royal Observatory in Greenwich, England. All other meridians are measured westward or eastward from the prime meridian.

Projection: A representation of the curved surface of the Earth on a flat surface such as a map.

Reef: A ridge of rocks or coral at or near the surface of the water. An **atoll** is a coral reef that encircles a body of water. A **barrier reef** is a coral reef separated from land by a deep lagoon. A **fringing reef** is a coral reef attached to an island.

Ria shoreline: A coast formed when seawater submerges land that is cut by numerous long and narrow river valleys.

Rill: A very small stream of water, often forming part of the headwaters of a river.

River: A freshwater surface stream of considerable volume running from higher to lower ground and draining into the sea, a lake, or another river.

Savanna: An expansive grassland that supports drought-resistant trees and undergrowth.

Scarp: A line of cliffs created by faulting or erosion.

Sediment: An accumulation of tiny pieces of rock, minerals, or organic matter, deposited by water, wind, or glaciers.

Sedimentary rock: Rock formed from layers of sediment that have been compacted and cemented together; along with igneous and metamorphic rock, it is one of the three major rock types.

Shoal: A shallow mound of sand or mud just beneath the surface of a body of water.

Soil: The topmost part of Earth's crust; it has been acted upon by physical, chemical, or biological agents so that it can support rooted plants.

Stalactite: An icicle-shaped deposit of calcium carbonate that hangs from the roof of a cave.

Stalagmite: A cone-shaped deposit of calcium carbonate that rises above the floor of a cave.

Steppes: A vast, treeless, grassy plain that covers the arid regions of southeastern Europe and Asia.

Subsidence: The sinking or lowering of part of Earth's surface.

Surveying: The branch of mathematics that determines the area of any portion of the Earth's surface, the lengths and directions of the area's boundary lines, and the area's surface contours.

Telemeter: Any instrument that uses a laser beam, sound waves, or light to measure the distance between an object and the observer.

Temperate zone: In the Northern Hemisphere, the area of mild climates between the Tropic of Cancer (about 23½° north latitude) and the Arctic Circle; in the Southern Hemisphere, the area of mild climates between the Tropic of Capricorn (about 23½° south latitude) and the Antarctic Circle.

Terrace: A flat area, with a vertical or sloping front or sides, that enables crops to be grown on hills. Also, naturally occurring flat or gently sloped areas along a riverbank or seacoast.

Topography: The physical features of a parcel of land, especially its elevations and depressions.

Trade wind: A wind that blows almost constantly from the east at 30° latitude north and south of the equator.

Tributary: A stream that empties into a larger stream or river, or into a lake.

Tropics: The region lying between the Tropic of Cancer (about 23½° north latitude) and the Tropic of Capricorn (about 23½° south latitude).

Tundra: A treeless plain, common in the subarctic and arctic regions of North America, Europe, and Asia, with black, mucky topsoil and a permanently frozen subsoil.

Vapor: The gaseous state of a liquid or solid, most commonly of water.

Wadi: A riverbed that is dry except during the rainy season, when it floods or gives rise to an oasis. Usually applied to rivers in southwest Asia and north Africa.

Index

River's, 34, *35*
Drowned valleys, *90-91*
Drumlins, glaciers' formation of, *44-45*
Dryland farming, 138
Dunes: formation of, *108-109;* Sahara's, *100-101, 105, 109*

E

Echo sounder, survey ship using, *18*
Egypt: Nile, *4-5, 33;* Sahara, *100-101*
England: Greenwich meridian, *21;* London, *116,* 128; Thames River, *38*
Equal-area map projection, *17*
Erosion: in Appalachian Mountains' formation, *96-97;* aquifers exposed by, *62, 63;* cuestas formed by, *92-93;* by Himalayan rivers, *98-99;* of limestone, *58-59;* marine, effects of, *68-69, 76-77, 88-89;* Monument Valley's formation by, *110-111;* plains formed by, *28, 29;* and terraces, *88-89*
Erosional plains, *28, 29*
Eskers, *66;* formation of, *44, 67*
Estuaries, *38-39*
Evaporation in global water cycle, 68, 82; vs. precipitation, *83*

F

Farming. *See* Agriculture
Fault-block mountains, *86*
Fiji, *21*
Finland, landscape formation in, *66-67*
Firn zone of Alps, 142, *chart* 142
Fishing areas, *126-127*
Fjords, *91*
Flooding of rivers: and alluvial fans, *30-31;* and estuaries, *39;* Yellow, *34*
Flood plains, *27;* of Mississippi, *29*
Flood tides: and estuaries, *38;* South American, *36, 37*
Flow (landslide), *103*
Fontana Dam, N.C., power station, *134*
Forests, lumber exports from, 124, *maps* 124-125, *125*
France: beach, Normandy, *68-69;* cuestas, *93;* temperature, Paris's, *chart* 116
Fringing reefs, *81*
Fuji, Mount, Japan, *22-23*

G

Glaciers, 24, *52-53;* Columbia Icefield, *24-25;* Finland, effect on, *66-67;* and fjord formation, *91;* formation of, *42-43;* Great Lakes formed by, *48-49;* landforms created by, *44-45, 46-47;* melting, possible, effects of, *72-73;*

Pleistocene glaciations, *charts* 50, *maps* 51
Global warming, mechanism of, *73*
Globe, Martin Behaim's, *14*
Gobi Desert, China-Mongolia: effect of ice ages on, *51;* oasis in, *63*
Grain production, *122-123*
Grand Canyon, Ariz., *84-85, 94-95*
Grape growing, *136-137;* roots, *137*
Grassland, African (savanna), *113*
Great Barrier Reef, Australia, *80-81*
Great circles, *17, 21*
Great Lakes, Canada-U.S., formation of, *48-49*
Great Plains, Canada-U.S., *29;* wheat crop, *123*
Greenhouse gases, buildup of, *73*
Greenwich, England, prime meridian at, *21*
Ground moraine, *46*
Ground subsidence, *64-65*
Ground water, 54; and caverns, *54-55, 59, 60-61;* landscape shaped by, *58-59;* movement of, gravity and, *56-57;* and oases, *62-63;* overpumping of, and subsidence, *64-65*
Guilin, China, tower karst of, *59*
Gyoki Bosatsu, map by, *15*
Gyres (circular currents), 70, *71*

H

Himalayas (mountains), Asia, rivers crossing, *98-99*
Hokkaido (island), Japan, sand spit on, *75*
Honshu (island), Japan, mountain on, *22-23*
Horns, glacial, *44*
Hundred Dishes (terraced pools), Akiyoshi Cave, Japan, *54-55*

I

Ice ages, 50, *charts* 50, *maps* 51; vs. interglacial periods, effect of, on deserts, *51, 106-107;* melting after, and estuaries, 38
Icecaps, polar, *52-53;* changes in, effect of, on deserts, *106-107;* melting, possibility of, *72-73*
Ice sheets. *See* Glaciers
Ijssel, Lake, the Netherlands, 133
India, collision of, with Asia, *98-99*
Influent streams, formation of, *30-31*
Inlets: drowned valleys with, *90;* and sand bar formation, *74-75*
International Date Line, *20, 21*
Irkutsk, Russia, climate of, *117*

Irrigation, *138-139;* kanats for, *63, 139;* with Yellow River water, *35*
Islands: Antarctic, *52-53;* coastal terraces around, *89;* coral reefs around, *80-81;* drowned valleys with, *90*
Italy: agriculture, *131, map* 137; climate, *chart* 137; Tiber River delta, *33*
Iwaki, Japan, *77*

J

Japan: airport construction, *144;* Akiyoshi Cave, *54-55;* alluvial fan, *31;* computer mapping, *22-23;* delta, *26;* Fuji, Mount, *22-23;* Gyoki map of, *15;* Iwaki, *77;* landslide, *103;* Notsukezaki, Cape, *75;* subsidence, *65;* terraces, *89;* V-shaped canyon, *26*
Jasper National Park, Canada, *24-25*
Jizuki, Mount, Japan, landslide on, *103*

K

Kaibab Plateau, Ariz., *95*
Kanats, *63, 139*
Karrens, formation of, *58-59*
Karst topography, *58;* development, *58-59*
Katashina River, Japan, terraces, *89*
Kauai (island), Hawaii, rainfall on, *115*
Kekaha, Hawaii, rainfall on, *115*
Kurobe Canyon, Japan, *26*

L

Lagoons, formation of: by coral reefs, *80-81;* by sand ridges, *74*
Lakes: artificial, for irrigation, *138;* Burley Griffin, Canberra, *128, map* 129; Finland's, formation of, *66-67;* Great Lakes, formation of, *48-49;* Ijssel, the Netherlands, 133; oxbow, formation of, *26-27;* Titicaca, Bolivia-Peru, *140, 141*
Landfill, airport constructed on, *144*
Land reclamation, *132-133*
Landslides, *102-103*
La Paz, Bolivia, *141;* climate, *chart* 140
Laser telemeters, *8-9*
Lateral moraines, *44, 46-47*
Latitude, 10, *11;* on Mercator projection, *16*
Laurentian Plateau, Canada, *29*
Leveling, surveyors' use of, 8, *9*
Life expectancy and population, 120
Limestone: caverns, *54-55, 59, 60-61;* karst topography, formation of, *58-59;* shoreline, cliffs along, *68-69*
Little Tennessee River, U.S., power station on, *134*

Staff for
UNDERSTANDING SCIENCE & NATURE

Assistant Managing Editor: Patricia Daniels
Editorial Directors: Allan Fallow, Karin Kinney
Writer: Mark Galan
Assistant Editor/Research: Elizabeth Thompson
Editorial Assistants: Louisa Potter, Marike van der Veen
Production Manager: Prudence G. Harris
Senior Copyeditor: Juli Duncan
Production: Celia Beattie
Library: Louise D. Forstall
Computer Composition: Deborah G. Tait (Manager), Monika D.
   Thayer, Janet Barnes Syring, Lillian Daniels

Special Contributors: Marfé Ferguson Delano, Barbara Mallen,
   Greg Mock, Lynn Yorke (text); James Graham, NOAA; James
   C. Luzius, Defense Mapping Agency (cartography)
Design/Illustration: Antonio Alcalá, Nicholas Fasciano, Al Kettler,
   David Neal Wiseman
Photography: Credits from left to right are separated by semicolons,
   from top to bottom by dashes. Cover: John Lewis Stage/The Im-
   age Bank. 1: Paolo Curto/The Image Bank. 4, 5: GEOPIC®,
   Earth Satellite Corporation. 6: U.S. Geological Survey (2).
   7: U.S. Geological Survey (top right). 9: Art by Al Kettler (top
   right). 10: Dennis di Cicco (top left). 18, 19: Maps and photo
   courtesy James Graham, NOAA. 20, 21: Globe art by Al Kettler;
   Dennis di Cicco (top center). 22: © Michael Freeman/Bruce Coleman, Inc., New York. 35: Lowell Georgia/Photo Researchers,
   New York. 38: Photo © Chesapeake Bay Foundation/EOSAT.
   40: Benn Mitchell/The Image Bank (top left). 48: Satellite image
   data processing by the Environmental Research Institute of
   Michigan (ERIM), Ann Arbor, Michigan. 52: Harald Sund/The
   Image Bank. 63: Guido Alberto Rossi/The Image Bank. 64: Art
   by Time-Life Books. 65: Art by Time-Life Books—© M. Timo-
   thy O'Keefe/Bruce Coleman, Inc., New York (bottom left).
   81: © Nicholas Devore III/Bruce Coleman, Inc., New York (bottom right). 86, 87: Jake Rajs/The Image Bank—Art by Nicholas
   Fasciano (3). 91: Per Eide/The Image Bank. 93: Alain Choisnet/
   The Image Bank. 96: James H. Carmichael, Jr./The Image Bank.
   117: Marc Romanelli/The Image Bank—Co Rentmeester/The
   Image Bank (middle photo). 123: Keith Philpott/The Image Bank
   (right). 128: Art by Al Kettler—© Ken Stepnell/Bruce Coleman,
   Inc., New York. 129: Art by Al Kettler. 131: © Jean-Claude
   Carton/Bruce Coleman, Inc., New York—Colin Molyneux/The
   Image Bank—Jake Rajs/The Image Bank (left); Giuliano Colliva/
   The Image Bank (right). 133: Bullaty Lomeo/The Image Bank
   (bottom right). 138: Grafton Marshall Smith/The Image Bank
   (bottom right). 141: Cara Moore/The Image Bank; © Pam
   Taylor/Bruce Coleman, Inc., New York—Fred Ihrt/The Image
   Bank; Nevada Wier/The Image Bank.
Research: Barbara Beroth
Index: Barbara L. Klein

Consultant:
   Dr. George Stephens is chairman of the geology department at
   The George Washington University in Washington, D.C. He
   specializes in mountain-building processes and the evolution of
   glacial landscapes.

TIME-LIFE for CHILDREN ®

Publisher: Robert H. Smith
Associate Publisher and Managing Editor: Neil Kagan
Assistant Managing Editor: Patricia Daniels
Editorial Directors: Jean Burke Crawford, Allan Fallow,
   Karin Kinney, Sara Mark, Elizabeth Ward
Director of Marketing: Margaret Mooney
Product Managers: Cassandra Ford, Amy Haworth,
   Shelley L. Schimkus
Director of Finance: Lisa Peterson
Financial Analyst: Patricia Vanderslice
Publishing Assistant: Marike van der Veen
Administrative Assistant: Barbara A. Jones

Original English translation by International Editorial Services Inc./
C. E. Berry

First printing. Printed in U.S.A.
Published simultaneously in Canada.
Time Life Inc. is a wholly owned subsidiary of
THE TIME INC. BOOK COMPANY.
TIME-LIFE is a trademark of Time Warner Inc. U.S.A.
For subscription information, call 1-800-621-7026.

Geography/editors of Time-Life Books.
        p.   cm. — (Understanding science & nature)
   Includes index.
   Summary: Questions and answers explore various aspects of
geography, including the formation of deserts, mountains, caves,
and rivers.
   ISBN 0-8094-9691-7 (trade) — ISBN 0-8094-9692-5 (lib. bdg.)
   1. Geography—Juvenile literature.
[1. Geography—Miscellanea.
2. Questions and answers.]
I. Series.
G175.G47   1993
910—dc20   92-34976
                                                                      CIP
                                                                      AC

DATE DUE

#47-0108 Peel Off Pressure Sensitive